DELIA'S
SUMMER COLLECTION

Photographs by Peter Knab

This book is published to accompany the
television series entitled *Delia Smith's Summer Collection*
which was produced by Hawkshead Ltd for the BBC
and first broadcast in May 1993.

Published by BBC Worldwide Ltd,
Woodlands, 80 Wood Lane
London W12 0TT
First published 1993
Reprinted 1993 (twelve times)
Reprinted 1994 (three times)
Reprinted 1995 (four times)
Reprinted 1996 (five times)
Reprinted 1997
Reprinted 1998
Reprinted 2000 (twice)
Reprinted 2001
First published in paperback 2003
Reprinted 2003
© Delia Smith 1993
The moral right of the author has been asserted.
ISBN 0 563 36476 9 (hardback)
ISBN 0 563 48870 0 (paperback)

Designed by Elaine Partington with Sara Kidd
Photographs by Peter Knab
Food preparation by Catherine Calland and special thanks to
Mary Cox for her help with the recipe testing
Illustrations by Vicky Emptage

Set in Monotype Baskerville by Selwood Systems, Midsomer Norton
Printed and bound in Great Britain by Butler & Tanner Ltd, Frome, Somerset
Colour separation by Radstock Reproductions Ltd, Midsomer Norton
Cover printed by Lawrence Allen Ltd, Weston-super-Mare

CONTENTS

Conversion Tables

All these are approximate conversions, which have either been rounded up or down. In a few recipes it has been necessary to modify them very slightly. Never mix metric and imperial measures in one recipe, stick to one system or the other. All spoon measurements used throughout this book are level unless specified otherwise.

OVEN TEMPERATURES

Mark 1	275°F	140°C
2	300	150
3	325	170
4	350	180
5	375	190
6	400	200
7	425	220
8	450	230
9	475	240

MEASUREMENTS

1/8 inch	3 mm
1/4	5 mm
1/2	1 cm
3/4	2
1	2.5
1 1/4	3
1 1/2	4
1 3/4	4.5
2	5
2 1/2	6
3	7.5
3 1/2	9
4	10
5	13
5 1/4	13.5
6	15
6 1/2	16
7	18
7 1/2	19
8	20
9	23
9 1/2	24
10	25.5
11	28
12	30

WEIGHTS

1/2 oz	10 g
3/4	20
1	25
1 1/2	40
2	50
2 1/2	60
3	75
4	110
4 1/2	125
5	150
6	175
7	200
8	225
9	250
10	275
12	350
1 lb	450
1 1/2	700
2	900
3	1.35 kg

VOLUME

2 fl oz	55 ml
3	75
5 (1/4 pt)	150
1/2 pt	275
3/4	425
1	570
1 1/4	725
1 3/4	1 litre
2	1.2
2 1/2	1.5
4	2.25

Introduction

'**Y**ou'll never be able to follow *Christmas*,' said a friend after my last book and television series. 'It's such a special time for people who cook, and whatever you do now it won't have that same magic.'

Well, I've always been the kind of person who loves a challenge, so here I am. A hard act to follow it may be, but Christmas comes and then it goes, leaving us with a whole year in between. Of course, none of us, I suspect, would care to indulge ourselves in quite the same way more than once a year. But moods, like seasons, change and the anticipation of something new and different is what gives life an edge.

Summer, in my opinion, is an equally special time for cooks, a dazzling time when fresh ingredients present themselves in rapid succession, some of them so briefly that we need to snap them up to enjoy them at their best. No-one would deny that we live in a privileged age when we can shop all round the world for anything at any time of the year, but that should never eclipse the joy of being able to eat something grown here at home when it's at its peak. Nature, with its changing seasons, varies our diet beautifully and can – if we allow it – relieve us of some of those agonising decisions which come from having too much choice.

This book and its accompanying series will take us on a journey, beginning with the early asparagus, garden rhubarb and gooseberries of May, through to the last of the runner beans pickled in August and ready for winter. I would also add that, while we are following the season closely, we are not confined to specifically British recipes: we are tracking summer round the world for new ideas and inspiration.

If the British summer proves to be a little elusive, fear not, it has been captured and held for you in the following pages. Peter Knab's dazzling photographs and what I think are the sunniest recipes I've ever cooked will, I hope, help to cheer up the cloudiest of days.

Have a happy summer.

Delia Smith

CHAPTER ONE

SOUPS, STARTERS
and
LIGHT LUNCH
DISHES

———— ◊ ————

Everything in this chapter is suitable in smaller portions as a first course, or for a light summer's lunch in larger portions – and that includes the soups. One thing I've found a certain resistance – not to say closed minds – to over the years is chilled soup. There are several here and I would like to make a case for them. Perhaps because of the climate the British traditionally think of soups as warming and comforting, and chilling them therefore seems a contradiction in terms. Yet nothing is as refreshing on a warm day as, say, a gaspacho, which I always think of as salad soup, a way of sipping and savouring all the fragrance of a salad. The antipathy arises, I'm sure, because of the British trait of never quite chilling anything properly. If a cold soup is meant to be refreshing, then it has *got* to be really cold and not, as we have often found in restaurants, tepid! Anyway, for those who remain unconverted let me say that all the soups in this chapter taste good served hot.

If you're looking for a light vegetarian lunch, may I draw your attention to the Fried Halloumi Cheese with Lime and Caper Vinaigrette which is every bit as delicious as it looks in the photograph on page 17, and the Piedmont Roasted Peppers (page 12) which are so good that nobody can ever believe they are so simple to make. One final thought – as a change from butter, how about putting a bowl of Provençale Tapenade (page 19) on the table to spread on a selection of breads to nibble before the main part of a meal arrives?

Chilled Fennel Gaspacho

·

SERVES 4

I've always loved gaspacho and never fail to order it when I'm in Spain or Portugal: it really is one of the nicest first courses when the weather is warm. This version is the same but different – the same refreshing, salady texture but quite a different flavour. This can be served warm if the weather's chilly, but if you are serving it cold, do make sure that it's really cold. Chill the bowls first and add some ice cubes just before serving.

1 largish fennel bulb	1 tablespoon extra virgin olive oil
1½ lb (700 g) ripe red tomatoes	¾ teaspoon chopped fresh oregano
1 small onion, chopped	1 teaspoon tomato purée
1 large clove garlic, crushed	1 rounded teaspoon rock salt
¾ teaspoon coriander seeds	
½ teaspoon mixed peppercorns	**TO GARNISH:**
1 tablespoon balsamic vinegar	Olive Croûtons (see page 15)
1 tablespoon lemon juice	

First skin the tomatoes. Pour boiling water over them and leave them for exactly 1 minute before draining them and slipping off the skins (protect your hands with a cloth if they're too hot). Then chop the tomatoes roughly.

Next trim the green fronds from the fennel (reserve these for a garnish) and cut the bulb into quarters. Trim away a little of the central stem at the base and slice the fennel into thinnish slices. Now place these in a saucepan with a little salt and measure in 15 fl oz (425 ml) of water. Bring it up to simmering point, then put a lid on and simmer gently for 10 minutes.

Meanwhile crush the coriander seeds and peppercorns in a pestle and mortar. Then heat the oil in a large saucepan and add the crushed spices along with the chopped onion. Let these cook gently for 5 minutes, then add the crushed garlic and cook for a further 2 minutes. Now add the balsamic vinegar, lemon juice, chopped tomatoes and oregano, stir well, then add the fennel along with the water in which it was simmering. Finally stir in the tomato purée, bring everything up to simmering point and simmer gently (without a lid) for 30 minutes.

After that whizz it all to a purée in a food processor or blender, or press it through a sieve. Then cool, cover and chill for several hours. Serve as described above, garnished with Olive Croûtons and the chopped green fennel fronds.

———— ◊ ————

Piedmont Roasted Peppers

·

SERVES 4 AS A STARTER

This recipe is quite simply stunning: hard to imagine how something so easily prepared can taste so good. Its history is colourful too. It was first discovered by Elizabeth David and published in her splendid book Italian Food. *Then the Italian chef Franco Taruschio at the Walnut Tree Inn near Abergavenny cooked it there. Simon Hopkinson, who ate it at the Walnut Tree, put it on his menu at his great London restaurant Bibendum, where I ate it – which is how it comes to be here now for you to make and enjoy.*

4 large red peppers (green are not suitable)

4 medium tomatoes

8 tinned anchovy fillets, drained

2 cloves garlic

8 dessertspoons Italian extra virgin olive oil

freshly milled black pepper

TO SERVE:
1 small bunch fresh basil leaves

For this it is essential to use a good, solid, *shallow* roasting-tray 16 × 12 inches (40 × 30 cm) (see page 194): if the sides are too deep, the roasted vegetables won't get those lovely, nutty, toasted edges.

Pre-heat the oven to gas mark 4, 350°F (180°C).

Begin by cutting the peppers in half and removing the seeds but leaving the stalks intact (they're not edible but they do look attractive and they help the pepper halves to keep their shape). Lay the pepper halves in a lightly oiled roasting-tray. Now put the tomatoes in a bowl and pour boiling water over them. Leave them for 1 minute, then drain them and slip the skins off, using a cloth to protect your hands. Then cut the tomatoes in quarters and place two quarters in each pepper half.

After that snip one anchovy fillet per pepper half into rough pieces and add to the tomatoes. Peel the garlic cloves, slice them thinly and divide the slices equally among the tomatoes and anchovies. Now spoon 1 dessertspoon of olive oil into each pepper, season with freshly milled pepper (but no salt because of the anchovies) and place the tray on a high shelf in the oven for the peppers to roast for 50 minutes–1 hour.

Then transfer the cooked peppers to a serving-dish, with all the precious juices poured over, and garnish with a few scattered basil leaves. These do need good bread to go with them as the juices are sublime. Focaccia with olive (page 214) would be perfect.

———— ◊ ————

Piedmont Roasted Peppers

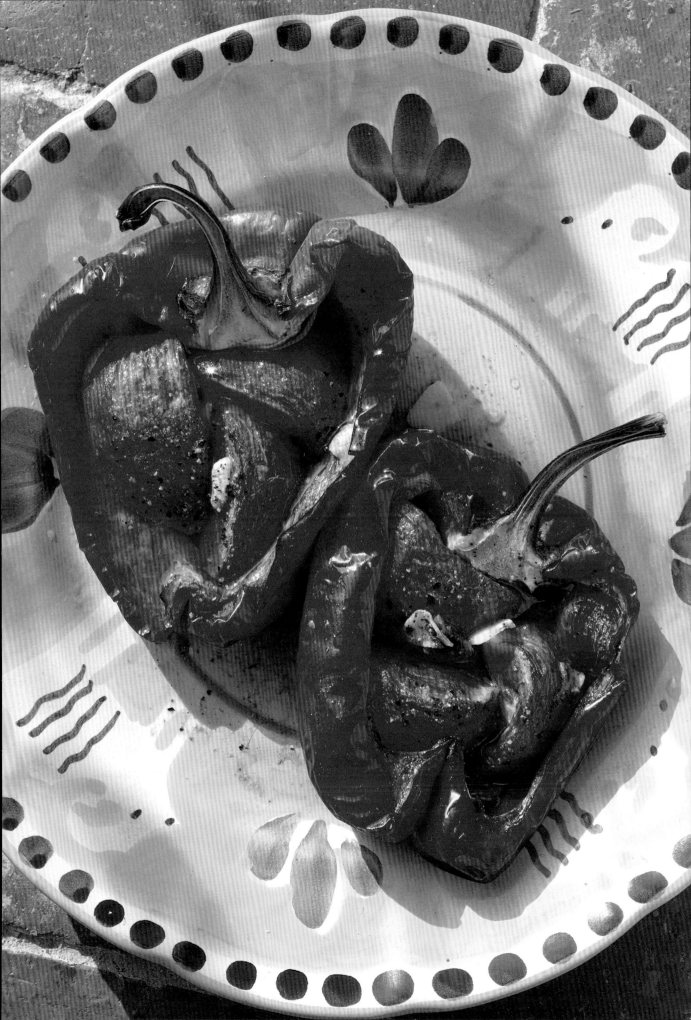

Roasted Tomato Soup *with a* Purée *of* Basil

·

SERVES 4

*A*t first you're going to think, 'Why bother to roast tomatoes just for a soup?', but I promise you that once you've tasted the difference you'll know it's worth it – and roasting really isn't any trouble, it just means time in the oven.

1½ lb (700 g) ripe red tomatoes
1 fat clove garlic, chopped
1 small bunch fresh basil leaves
1 × 4 oz (110 g) potato
15 fl oz (425 ml) boiling water
1 heaped teaspoon tomato purée
1 teaspoon balsamic vinegar
approx. 3 tablespoons extra virgin olive oil
salt and freshly milled black pepper

TO GARNISH:
Olive Croûtons (see page 15)

You will also need a solid, shallow roasting-tray approx. 13 × 13 inches (33 × 33 cm) – see page 194.

Pre-heat the oven to gas mark 5, 375°F (190°C).

First of all skin the tomatoes by pouring boiling water over them, then leave them for 1 minute exactly before draining them and slipping off the skins (protect your hands with a cloth if necessary). Now slice each tomato in half, arrange the halves on the roasting-tray, cut side uppermost, and season with salt and pepper. Sprinkle a few droplets of olive oil on to each one followed by the chopped garlic, and finally top each one with a piece of basil leaf (dipping the basil in oil first to get a good coating).

Now pop the whole lot into the oven and roast the tomatoes for 50 minutes–1 hour or until the edges are slightly blackened – what happens in this process is that the liquid in the tomatoes evaporates and concentrates their flavour, as do the toasted edges. About 20 minutes before the end of the roasting time, peel and chop the potato, place it in a saucepan with some salt, 15 fl oz (425 ml) of boiling water and the tomato purée and simmer for 20 minutes.

When the tomatoes are ready, remove them from the oven and scrape them with all their juices and crusty bits into a food processor (a spatula is best for this), then add the contents of the potato saucepan and whizz everything to a not-too-uniform purée. If you want to, you can now sieve out the seeds but I prefer to leave them in as I like the texture.

Just before serving the soup – which should be re-heated very gently – make the basil purée by stripping the leaves into a mortar, sprinkling with ¼ teaspoon of salt, then bashing the leaves down with the pestle. It takes a minute or two for the leaves to collapse down and become a purée, at which point add 2 tablespoons of olive oil and the balsamic vinegar and stir well.

(If you make this in advance, store it in a cup with clingfilm pressed on to the surface; it will keep its colour even overnight.) To serve the soup, pour it into warmed serving-bowls and drizzle the basil purée on to the surface, giving a marbled effect. Then finally sprinkle with Olive Croûtons and serve straight away.

◊

Olive Croûtons (Ciabatta)

4 medium slices ciabatta bread, weighing approx. 2 oz (50 g) each

1 tablespoon olive oil

1 dessertspoon olive paste (available from supermarkets)

Pre-heat the oven to gas mark 5, 375°F (190°C).

First of all cut the slices of bread into small cubes, then place them in a bowl together with the olive oil and olive paste and stir them around to get a good coating of both. Then arrange the croûtons on a small baking-sheet and put them in the oven to bake for 8–10 minutes – but please do put on a timer for this as 10 minutes pass very quickly and croûtons have a nasty habit of turning into cinders! Then leave to cool on the baking-sheet and serve with Chilled Fennel Gaspacho (page 11) or Roasted Tomato Soup (page 14).

◊

Fried Halloumi Cheese
with Lime *and* Caper Vinaigrette

·

SERVES 2 AS A LIGHT LUNCH OR 4 AS A STARTER

This is a great recipe to have up your sleeve for the unexpected vegetarian. Greek halloumi arrives in sealed plastic wrapping and has a reasonably long shelf-life, which means that you can always have a pack tucked away in the refrigerator. If you can get hold of some Greek olive oil for the dressing and eat this outside in the sunshine, the scent and the flavours will transport you to the Aegean in moments.

1 halloumi cheese	**1 heaped teaspoon grain mustard**
2 tablespoons well-seasoned flour	**1 heaped tablespoon chopped fresh**
2 tablespoons olive oil	**coriander leaves**
	2 tablespoons extra virgin olive oil
FOR THE DRESSING:	**salt and freshly milled black**
juice and zest of 1 lime	**pepper**
1 tablespoon white wine vinegar	
1 heaped tablespoon capers, drained	**TO GARNISH:**
1 clove garlic, finely chopped	**a few sprigs of coriander**

First of all unwrap the cheese and pat it dry with kitchen paper. Then, using a sharp knife, slice it into eight slices, including the ends. Now prepare the dressing by simply whisking all the ingredients together in a small mixing-bowl.

When you're ready to serve the halloumi, heat the oil in a frying-pan over a medium heat. When the oil is really hot, press each slice of cheese into seasoned flour to coat it on both sides, then add them to the hot pan as they are done – they take 1 minute on each side to cook, so by the time the last one's in it will almost be time to turn the first one over. They need to be a good golden colour on each side.

Serve them straight away on warmed plates with the dressing poured over. This is good served with lightly toasted pitta bread or Greek bread with toasted sesame seeds.

———————— ◊ ————————

Fried Halloumi Cheese with Lime and Caper Vinaigrette

Chilled Lemon Grass *and* Coriander Vichyssoise

·

SERVES 4

*I*n summer, if the weather is really hot, nothing could be more refreshing than a chilled soup. Leeks, which have made this particular recipe famous, are not available in summer, but this alternative is, I think, even better. It's made using fresh lemon grass available at oriental shops and some of the larger supermarkets. Once again, remember to serve the soup well chilled.

2 medium onions, chopped	**4 thick stems lemon grass**
2 oz (50 g) butter	**4 spring onions, finely chopped**
2 oz (50 g) fresh coriander leaves	**salt and freshly milled black pepper**
10 oz (275 g) new potatoes, scraped and chopped small	
1½ pints (850 ml) stock (see below)	**TO GARNISH:**
5 fl oz (150 ml) milk	**thin lemon slices**

First of all strip the coriander leaves from the stalks and reserve the stalks. Lemon grass is dealt with in exactly the same way as leeks: that is, you trim the root and the tough top away, leaving approximately 6 inches (15 cm) of stem, remove the outer skin and chop the lemon grass quite finely. Then do the same with the spring onions. Next gather up all the trimmings from both, wash them and pop them into a saucepan together with the coriander stalks, some salt and 1½ pints (850 ml) of water and simmer (covered) for about 30 minutes to make a stock.

To make the soup, melt the butter in a large saucepan, then add the chopped lemon grass, onions (reserve the spring onions till later) and potatoes and keeping the heat low, let the vegetables sweat gently (covered) for about 10 minutes. After that pour in the stock through a strainer, discard the debris, then add the milk and about three-quarters of the coriander leaves. Season with salt and pepper, bring the soup up to simmering point and simmer very gently for about 25 minutes.

Allow the soup to cool a little before pouring it into a food processor or blender, whizz it up, then pour it through a strainer into a bowl. When it's cold, cover and chill thoroughly till you're ready to serve. I think it's a good idea to serve the soup in glass bowls that have already been chilled. Add a cube of ice to each bowl and sprinkle in the rest of the coriander (finely chopped) and the spring onions as a garnish. Finally float some lemon slices on top and serve straight away.

———————— ◊ ————————

Provençale Tapenade

.

SERVES 6

In the food markets in Provence there's always a dazzling stall piled with olives, shiny and glistening in the sun – black, green, purple, herbed, marinated and so on. Very often there is a tapenade stall as well, with any number of variations. Tapenade is a pungent olive paste made with anchovies and capers: perfect for outdoor eating with rough country bread and some chilled Provençale rosé.

1 × 14 oz (400 g) tin good-quality pitted black olives in brine, thoroughly drained	2 cloves garlic, crushed
	1 teaspoon Dijon mustard
	2 tablespoons extra virgin olive oil
3 oz (75 g) capers, drained and pressed between double layers of kitchen paper to absorb the surplus vinegar	2 teaspoons lemon juice
	2 tablespoons chopped fresh basil
	Freshly milled black pepper
1 × 2 oz (50 g) tin anchovy fillets in olive oil	

This is very simple to make. All you do is put the olives into a food processor along with the capers. Add the contents of the tin of anchovies (oil included) plus the garlic, mustard, olive oil, lemon juice and half the basil. Blend until the mixture is reduced to a spreadable paste, but not so finely that the pieces become unidentifiable (the olives need to be chopped just enough to resemble slightly large grains of sand). Then scrape the mixture into a small bowl, taste and season with freshly milled pepper (no salt because of the anchovies). Just before serving sprinkle in the remaining basil. Tapenade keeps for up to 2 weeks in a covered jar and can be used in a number of other ways: stir a spoonful into soup or a salad dressing, or use as a topping for baked croûtons.

———————— ◊ ————————

Fresh Asparagus
with Foaming Hollandaise

·

SERVES 4 AS A STARTER

The marriage of asparagus and hollandaise was quite definitely made in heaven, and it seems sad to me that 'health' issues should bring about a divorce. Therefore I have set out to lighten the sauce somewhat by the addition of stiffly beaten egg whites. I now actually prefer the golden foam to the classic all butter and egg yolk sauce.

1¼ lb (570 g) fresh asparagus stalks (medium thick)	FOR THE SAUCE:
	2 large eggs, separated
salt	1 dessertspoon white wine vinegar
	1 dessertspoon lemon juice
	4 oz (110 g) salted butter
	salt and freshly milled black pepper

You can make the sauce at any time: we have tried it chilled overnight in the refrigerator which makes a nice contrast with the hot asparagus, or you can serve it warm, or even at room temperature.

Begin by placing the egg yolks in a food processor or blender together with some salt, switch on and blend them thoroughly. In a small saucepan heat the lemon juice and vinegar till the mixture simmers, then switch the processor on again and pour the hot liquid on to the egg yolks in a steady stream.

Switch off, then in the same saucepan melt the butter – not too fiercely: it mustn't brown. When it is liquid and foaming, switch on the processor once more and pour in the butter, again in a steady thin stream, until it is all incorporated and the sauce has thickened. Next, in a small bowl, whisk the egg whites until they form soft peaks and then fold the sauce, a tablespoon at a time into the egg whites and taste to check the seasoning. When you've done that it's ready to serve or it can be left till later.

To cook the asparagus: take each stalk in both hands and bend and snap off the woody end, then trim with a knife to make it neater. Lay the asparagus stalks on an opened fan steamer (or an ordinary steamer will do) – they can be piled one on top of the other. Season with salt, place them in a frying-pan or saucepan, pour in about 1 inch (2.5 cm) of boiling water from the kettle, then put a lid on and steam for 4–6 minutes.

Serve the hot asparagus with some sauce poured over the tips, and don't forget to have finger-bowls and napkins at the ready.

———— ◊ ————

Fresh Asparagus with Foaming Hollandaise

Sautéed Asparagus *with* Eggs *and* Parmesan

·

SERVES 2

Asparagus has a wonderful affinity with egg and a hint of cheese, especially Parmesan. In this recipe it is sautéed to a nutty brown at the edges, sprinkled with a little balsamic vinegar and served with fried eggs, though you can poach them if you prefer. If you really want to have some fun, try little fried quail's eggs, which look so pretty and dainty with their lacy brown edges – like all eggs, though, they must be very fresh, so you need a reliable supplier. Just before serving scatter a few shavings of Parmesan over and you have an absolutely stunning summer lunch for two people.

8 oz (225 g) asparagus stalks (the thinner ones are best), trimmed as in the recipe on page 21	2 very fresh hen's eggs or 6 quail's eggs
2 tablespoons olive oil	1 tablespoon Parmesan shavings (see recipe)
1 tablespoon balsamic vinegar	salt and freshly milled black pepper

First prepare the Parmesan: for this you need a potato peeler to lightly shave off tiny slivers till you have approximately 1 tablespoon.

For this recipe you need two frying-pans. In the first one heat 1 tablespoon of olive oil over a high heat, add the asparagus stalks, then immediately turn the heat down to medium. Move the stalks about in the pan and turn them so that they are a little toasted at the edges (they should take 3–4 minutes to cook but this will depend on their thickness). When they're done, turn off the heat, add the balsamic vinegar and let them keep warm in the pan while you cook the eggs.

Heat 1 tablespoon of olive oil in the other frying-pan. Then, if you are using quail's eggs, make a small slit in the shells with a sharp (preferably serrated) knife – if you crack them like hen's eggs, the yolks will break. When the oil is hot, quickly break each egg into the pan, one after the other, then tilt the pan, baste the eggs with hot oil and after about 1 minute they will be done.

Arrange the asparagus on warmed serving-plates with the pan juices sprinkled over. Top each portion with 3 quail's eggs or 1 hen's egg, season with salt and freshly milled black pepper, sprinkle on the Parmesan and serve pronto!

———————— ◊ ————————

Asparagus *under* Wraps

·

SERVES 2 AS A LIGHT LUNCH OR 4 AS A STARTER

The asparagus in this dish is steamed lightly, then wrapped with cheese and Parma ham and baked till the cheese is melted. Italian fontina, if you can get it, has the right squidgy consistency, but the recipe also works well with the sharp flavour of Parmesan.

12 asparagus stalks (thick ones if possible)	**TO SERVE:** **grated Parmesan cheese**
6 oz (175 g) fontina or Parmesan cheese	**You will also need a solid baking-sheet, lightly oiled.**
12 slices Parma ham, total weight approx. 5 oz (150 g)	Pre-heat the oven to gas mark 6, 400°F (200°C).

To cook the asparagus: take each stalk in both hands and bend and snap off the woody end, then trim with a knife to make it neater. Lay the asparagus stalks on an opened fan steamer (or an ordinary steamer will do) – they can be piled one on top of the other. Season with salt, place them in a frying-pan or saucepan, pour in about 1 inch (2.5 cm) of boiling water from the kettle, then put a lid on and steam for 4–6 minutes.

If you're using fontina, slice it into thin strips using a sharp knife. If you're using Parmesan, coarsely grate it. Now lay the slices of Parma ham out flat on a work-surface, divide the strips of cheese along the centre of each slice of ham (or sprinkle with the grated Parmesan if using that), then simply lay an asparagus stalk at one end and roll the whole lot up fairly firmly.

All this can be done well in advance; then, when you're ready to cook, lay the rolls on the baking-sheet and pop on to the highest shelf of the oven for just 5 minutes, or until the cheese begins to melt. Serve piping hot with a little grated Parmesan to sprinkle over.

———————— ◊ ————————

CHAPTER TWO

HERBS, SALADS
and
DRESSINGS

———— ◊ ————

ince I last wrote on this particular subject things have progressed beyond any expectation. I'll let you into a secret: when I first started writing recipes, olive oil was something sold in medicine-type bottles in Boots the Chemist, and the post-war British salad was still being heavily laced with bottled salad cream.

Not so now. Salad leaves daily get more and more exotic, and oils and vinegars come in every shape, size and flavour. You can buy Greek olive oil to go in a Greek dish – or French, Italian or Spanish likewise. Then there are herb oils and fruit vinegars, a bewildering array and – dare I say it? – a little over the top for most of us. Unless I'm regularly making a recipe that calls for, say, strawberry vinegar all it does is sit there taking up valuable houseroom awaiting that special need that never arises. After early-summer experiments with a whole range of herb-infused oils we found at the end of the day that they simply lined up unused (with one exception, basil oil, which came into its own in winter when there were no basil plants in the house). One of the glories of summer is the profusion of herbs, so if you want their flavour use them fresh – there's no need for oils.

For something new in salads can I urge you to try the Pesto Rice Salad, a cross between a salad and a risotto? Another winner is the Grilled Spanish Onion with Rocket-leaf Salad (page 34), and the Mixed-leaf Caesar Salad on page 28 is, I may say with all modesty, the best I've tasted to date!

Middle Eastern Tabouleh Salad

·

SERVES 6–8 AS A SIDE SALAD

*T*his *Middle Eastern salad is so pretty and summery, and if you have mint in the garden which is growing as wild as a jungle – as mine does – it's a wonderful way to use some of it!*

8 oz (225 g) cracked wheat (available from health-food shops)	**4 inches (10 cm) cucumber, very finely chopped**
2 oz (50 g) parsley, finely chopped	**4 tablespoons extra virgin olive oil**
8 spring onions, finely chopped (including the green parts)	**salt and freshly milled black pepper**
4 tablespoons lemon juice	
2 large beef tomatoes, approx. 1 lb (450 g)	**TO SERVE:**
1½ oz (40 g) fresh mint leaves without stalks, finely chopped	**crisp lettuce leaves**

Start off by measuring the cracked wheat into a bowl, cover it with plenty of cold water and leave for approximately 20 minutes or until the grains soften and lose their crunchiness (which means, of course, you'll have to bite a few to find out how they're going).

Then have ready a large sieve or colander lined with a clean tea-towel. When the cracked wheat has softened, pour the contents of the bowl into the sieve, drain and squeeze hard to extract as much water as possible. Shake the wheat into a deep bowl and stir in the parsley and spring onions followed by the lemon juice and 1½ teaspoons of salt to combine thoroughly. Then (if you have time) chill it in the refrigerator for 1 hour.

Meanwhile skin the tomatoes. Pour boiling water over them and leave for 1 minute, then slip off the skins, protecting your hands with a cloth if you need to. Halve the tomatoes and squeeze out the seeds before chopping the flesh quite small and adding to the bowl containing the wheat. Next add the mint, cucumber and olive oil to the salad and mix to combine everything. Taste and season with salt and pepper. Serve piled straight on a plate lined with some crisp lettuce leaves.

◊

Mixed-leaf Caesar Salad

·

SERVES 4 AS A LIGHT LUNCH OR 6 AS A STARTER

This must be one of the greatest salad recipes ever. It's traditionally made with Cos lettuce, but I like a mixture of Cos, Crispheart (Webb's) and some crunchy rocket leaves. What it can't take is anything too soft – only the crunchiest leaves will do. The flavours are gutsy, so it's ideal for a summer lunch outside or, in small portions, for a quite aristocratic but so-simple starter.

1 small Cos lettuce	**FOR THE DRESSING:**
1 packet prepared Crispheart lettuce (or the heart of a Webb's Wonder)	**1 × large egg**
	1 clove garlic
1 large handful rocket leaves	**juice of 1 lime**
1 × 2 oz (50 g) tin anchovy fillets, drained (keep the oil for the dressing)	**1 heaped teaspoon mustard powder**
	½ teaspoon Worcestershire sauce
	5 fl oz (150 ml) extra virgin olive oil
FOR THE CROÛTONS:	**1½ oz (40 g) Reggio Parmesan cheese, finely grated**
2 oz (50 g) crustless white bread, cut into ⅓-inch (8-mm) cubes	**salt and freshly milled black pepper**
1 tablespoon extra virgin olive oil	
1 rounded tablespoon finely grated Reggio Parmesan cheese	
1 clove garlic, crushed	**You will also need a baking-sheet.**

First make the croûtons. Pre-heat the oven to gas mark 4, 350°F (180°C), then place the cubes of bread in a bowl together with 1 tablespoon of olive oil and 1 rounded tablespoon of Parmesan plus the crushed clove of garlic. Stir and toss the bread round to get an even coating of cheese, oil and garlic, then spread the croûtons out on the baking-sheet and bake them on a high shelf in the oven for 10 minutes. Please put a kitchen timer on at this stage! I'm afraid I have burnt more croûtons than I care to remember simply because the 10 minutes went so quickly! When the buzzer goes, remove them from the oven and leave to cool.

Meanwhile make the dressing by breaking the egg into the bowl of a food processor and add the garlic (peeled but not crushed), the lime juice, 2 of the anchovy fillets, the mustard and Worcestershire sauce. Switch on and blend everything till smooth; then, keeping the motor running, pour the olive oil and anchovy oil (which can be combined in a jug first) through the feeder funnel in a slow, steady stream.

When all the oil is in you should have a slightly thickened, emulsified sauce with the consistency of pouring cream. Taste the dressing and season with

Mixed-leaf Caesar Salad

freshly milled black pepper and salt if it needs it.

Now arrange the lettuce leaves (breaking up the larger ones as you go) in a large, roomy salad bowl. After that snip in the remaining anchovies and mix to distribute them evenly among the leaves. When you're ready to serve, pour over the dressing and toss very thoroughly to coat all the leaves. Sprinkle in 1½ oz (40 g) Parmesan, toss again and finally scatter the croûtons over the salad. Then either portion it out or pass the bowl round for everyone to help themselves.

◇

Pitta Bread Salad

·

SERVES 4 AS A MAIN COURSE OR 6 AS A SIDE SALAD WITH BARBECUED MEAT OR FISH

*A*nother *Middle Eastern salad, originally called* fattoush, *this may sound unlikely, but it really is good. It's robust and chunky with the fresh flavours of herbs and lemon – and dead simple to make.*

2 standard-sized pitta breads	**4 spring onions, thinly sliced (including the green parts)**
1 small Cos lettuce, cut into ½-inch (1-cm) strips	**1 smallish red onion, chopped small**
2 largish tomatoes, skinned and cut into ½-inch (1-cm) cubes	**1 red, yellow or green pepper, de-seeded and chopped small**
4 inches (10 cm) unpeeled cucumber, cut into ½-inch (1-cm) cubes	
6 rounded tablespoons coarsely chopped parsley	**FOR THE LEMON DRESSING:**
	5 fl oz (150 ml) olive oil
1 × ½ oz (15 g) packet fresh mint leaves, snipped, or 2 heaped tablespoons chopped fresh garden mint	**zest of 1 lemon**
	4 tablespoons lemon juice
	salt and freshly milled black pepper

Pre-heat the grill to its highest setting.

In a large, roomy salad bowl combine the vegetables and chopped herbs and toss lightly to mix them evenly together. Then in another small bowl combine the ingredients for the dressing, whisk and season liberally. Spoon the dressing over the salad and toss again.

Now toast the pitta bread under the grill until it starts to get really crisp. Cut it into postage-stamp-sized pieces, scatter these into the salad and toss once more. Taste for seasoning and serve immediately.

———————— ◊ ————————

Roasted Tomato Salad

·

SERVES 4–6 AS A STARTER

If you are a tomato addict, like me, and you think that good bread dipped into fruity olive oil and tomato juices is the food of the gods, then roast the tomatoes first and you'll agree that the gods have excelled themselves.

12 large tomatoes
12 large fresh basil leaves
2 large or 4 small cloves garlic, finely chopped
2 tablespoons extra virgin olive oil
salt and freshly milled black pepper

FOR THE DRESSING:
2 tablespoons extra virgin olive oil
2 tablespoons balsamic vinegar

TO GARNISH:
12 large fresh basil leaves
24 black olives

You will also need a shallow roasting-tin approx. 16 × 12 inches (40 × 30 cm), oiled.

Pre-heat the oven to gas mark 6, 400°F (200°C).

Skin the tomatoes first of all by pouring boiling water over them and leaving for 1 minute, then drain and, as soon as they are cool enough to handle, slip off the skins. (Protect your hands with a cloth if necessary.) Now cut each tomato in half and place the halves in the roasting-tin (cut side uppermost) and season with salt and freshly milled pepper. After that sprinkle on the chopped garlic, distributing it evenly between the tomatoes. Follow this with a few droplets of olive oil on each one, then top each one with half a basil leaf, turning each piece of leaf over to get a coating of oil.

Now place the roasting-tin in the top half of the oven and roast the tomatoes for 50 minutes–1 hour or until the edges are slightly blackened. Then remove the tin from the oven and allow the tomatoes to cool. All this can be done several hours ahead.

To serve the tomatoes, transfer them to individual serving-plates, place half a basil leaf on top of each tomato half, then whisk the oil and balsamic vinegar together and drizzle this over the tomatoes. Finally top each one with an olive. Lots of crusty bread is an essential accompaniment to this.

———————— ◊ ————————

Roasted Tomato Salad

Grilled Spanish Onion *with* Rocket-leaf Salad

·

SERVES 4

I am constantly amazed after all my years of cooking at how there can be anything new – but there always is, and again and again. this is an example, utterly simple, yet quite unlike any other salad. If rocket leaves are unavailable, flat-leaf parsley with lamb's lettuce is a good substitute.

4 Spanish onions (the largest you can get)	**juice of 1 large lemon**
6–7 tablespoons extra virgin olive oil	**salt and freshly milled black pepper**
approx. 1 oz (25 g) rocket leaves or flat-leaf parsley and lamb's lettuce	**You will also need a grill pan lined with foil with a grill rack on top.**
3 oz (75 g) Reggio Parmesan cheese (in a piece)	Pre-heat the grill at its highest setting for about 5 minutes.

First of all, don't peel the onions: simply trim off the root and top before cutting each one across into four slices about ³/₄ inch (2 cm) thick. Keeping the slices whole, transfer them to the grill rack (you might have to do this in two batches, depending on the size of your grill), then brush them with oil and season with salt and freshly milled pepper. Now position the grill pan so that the onion slices are about 4 inches (10 cm) from the heat and grill for 7 or 8 minutes until the onions are browned – indeed within a whisker of being blackened.

While that's happening, prepare the Parmesan by shaving it into wafer-thin pieces with a potato peeler. For the onions the next stage needs a little care: use a palette knife to turn the slices over so that they don't break up into their constituent rings. Repeat the same oiling, seasoning and grilling on the other side, then remove from the heat and leave them on one side until they're cool enough to handle.

Now discard the outside layers and any parts of the onion slices that are too blackened or chewy to eat, and separate the cold onion into rings. Put about a quarter of the rings in a layer on a serving-dish and gradually build up the salad, intermingling onion rings with the torn rocket leaves and shavings of Parmesan, sprinkling with more salt and pepper, lemon juice and about 3 tablespoons of olive oil as you go. This salad should not be tossed, so it relies on the cook to mingle the ingredients as the salad is put together. Serve at room temperature.

———————— ◊ ————————

Home-made Pesto Sauce

.

SERVES 2–3 WITH PASTA

Every year I grow enough basil leaves to see me through the summer and, most importantly, to make at least one home-made pesto sauce. A lot of precious leaves are needed to make up 2 oz (50 g), but it really is worth it as the home-made version puts all the ready-made ones in the shade. If you can get Pecorino Romano it has a more gutsy flavour than Parmesan, but if you can't Parmesan will do well.

2 oz (50 g) fresh basil leaves	**1 oz (25 g) Pecorino Romano**
1 large clove garlic, crushed	**cheese, grated**
1 tablespoon pine kernels	**salt**
6 tablespoons extra virgin olive oil	

If you have a blender, put the basil, garlic, pine kernels and olive oil together with some salt in the goblet and blend until you have a smooth purée. Then transfer the purée to a bowl and stir in the grated Pecorino cheese.

If you don't have a blender, use a large pestle and mortar to pound the basil, garlic and pine kernels to a paste. Slowly add the salt and cheese, then very gradually add the oil until you have obtained a smooth purée.

———————— ◊ ————————

Pesto Rice Salad

·

SERVES 4–6

*J*ust *as home-made pesto does such wonders for pasta, so it does for rice too. This salad can be served warm as a first course and it's extremely good as an accompaniment to fish or chicken main-course dishes. Served cold it makes a lovely addition to a selection of salads for a buffet.*

Italian arborio rice measured to the 8 fl oz (225 ml) level in a glass measuring-jug	**4 spring onions, finely chopped**
	juice of 1 lemon
1 quantity Home-made Pesto Sauce (see page 35)	**2 tablespoons extra virgin olive oil**
	a few fresh basil leaves
16 fl oz (450 ml) boiling vegetable stock	**1 oz (25 g) Reggio Parmesan cheese shavings (made with a potato peeler)**
	salt and freshly milled black pepper

First of all measure the rice into a glass measuring-jug, then add about one quarter of the pesto sauce to it and stir it around to coat all the grains. Tip the mixture into a shallow saucepan or frying-pan with a lid and pour the boiling stock into the jug, then pour this over the rice. Now turn on the heat and stir with a wooden spoon, adding 1 teaspoon of salt. Then, when it begins to boil, put a lid on, turn the heat down to low and let the rice cook for exactly 20 minutes.

As soon as it's ready, tip all the rice into a serving-bowl, then simply pour in the lemon juice, olive oil and the remaining pesto sauce. Combine all the ingredients together, stirring and tossing. At this stage taste and season with salt and pepper. Finally scatter some torn basil leaves, finely chopped spring onion and then some shavings of Parmesan over the surface of the salad as a garnish. If you want to serve the salad cold, add the basil, onion and Parmesan just before serving.

──────── ◊ ────────

Pesto Rice Salad

Marinated Mozzarella *with* Avocado

·

SERVES 2 AS A SNACK LUNCH

*T*his is very pretty and very summery, but it is dependent on getting hold of good-quality mozzarella. Buffalo mozzarella is the best, but failing that the full-fat cheese made from cow's milk has a lovely creamy texture.

4 oz (110 g) mozzarella cheese	FOR THE VINAIGRETTE DRESSING:
1 medium ripe avocado	1 small clove garlic
strip of red pepper, 1 × 3 inches (2.5 × 7.5 cm)	1 level teaspoon rock salt
approx. 18 fresh basil leaves	1 rounded teaspoon mustard powder
2 spring onions, finely chopped	1 dessertspoon white wine vinegar
	5 dessertspoons extra virgin olive oil
	1 dessertspoon snipped fresh chives
	salt and freshly milled black pepper

Start to prepare the salad about 2 hours before you need it (but no longer as the cheese then begins to soften too much). Slice the mozzarella into $^{1}/_{4}$-inch (5-mm) slices; then halve the avocado, remove and discard the stone and skin, and thinly slice each half.

Now arrange the mozzarella and avocado on a serving-plate with alternate slices overlapping each other. Next slice the strip of red pepper into the finest shreds possible, starting from the narrow 1-inch (2.5-cm) end, then pile the basil leaves on top of each other and slice these into similar shreds and scatter both basil and pepper over the cheese and avocado. Make up the dressing by crushing the garlic and salt together with a pestle and mortar, and work the mustard powder into the puréed garlic and salt followed by plenty of freshly milled pepper. Stir in the vinegar, oil and chives, then pour the dressing into a screw-top jar and shake vigorously before pouring it over the other ingredients on the plate. Cover with an upturned plate or some foil and leave to marinate for 2 hours. Serve with ciabatta (olive oil bread).

———————— ◊ ————————

Tomato, Mozzarella *and* Basil Salad

·

SERVES 2

If you don't have time for a marinade as in the previous recipe, this variation makes a very quick, simple first course or light lunch salad.

4 oz (110 g) mozzarella cheese, sliced	**2 tablespoons Italian extra virgin**
approx. 24 fresh basil leaves	**olive oil**
1 lb (450 g) tomatoes	**salt and freshly milled black pepper**

First put the tomatoes in a bowl and pour boiling water over them. Leave them for 1 minute, then drain and slip the skins off using a cloth to protect your hands if necessary. Then slice the tomatoes thinly.

All you do now is arrange the slices of mozzarella and tomato in layers, either in rows or concentric circles, on a serving-dish. Scatter the whole basil leaves over them, then, just before serving, sprinkle with plenty of salt and freshly milled pepper and drizzle the olive oil all over. Serve with some ciabatta bread, warmed a little in the oven to the crispy stage.

———————— ◊ ————————

Fresh Crab Salad *in* Vinaigrette

·

SERVES 2

This is a very good recipe for using those small, ready-dressed crabs that are sold in the half-shell. The tartness of capers, gherkins and lime cut through the richness of the crab perfectly.

8 oz (225 g) mixed prepared crab meat (this is using 2 half-shells)	**2 tablespoons fresh lime juice**
2 large or 4 small cornichons (continental gherkins), finely chopped	**1 shallot, finely chopped**
	1 tablespoon white wine
1 tablespoon capers, drained and chopped	**1 tablespoon light olive oil**
(or, if they're small, leave them whole)	**a few drops of tabasco sauce**
1 tablespoon finely chopped fresh coriander leaves	**salt and freshly milled black pepper**
	TO GARNISH:
finely grated zest of 1 lime	**a few crisp salad leaves or some watercress**

It couldn't be simpler: all you do is combine all the ingredients in a bowl, then divide the mixture into two. Take each quantity, pile it on a plate and use your hands to form it into a round, flattened shape about $^1/_2$ inch (1 cm) high. Garnish with some crisp salad leaves or watercress all round and serve with some buttered brown bread. The wholegrain sunflower and poppy-seed loaf on page 219 goes particularly well with this.

———————— ◊ ————————

American Blue Cheese Dressing

·

SERVES 4–6

I love American salad dressings, and especially this one. The blue cheese can be Roquefort, if you want to splash out, or Danish Blue, which crumbles well: the only stipulation is that the cheese has to be gutsy. A subtle, faint-hearted cheese will get lost amongst all the other strong flavours.

5 fl oz (150 ml) soured cream	**2 tablespoons light olive oil**
2 tablespoons good mayonnaise	**1 tablespoon balsamic vinegar**
1 large or 2 small cloves garlic	**1 tablespoon lemon juice**
1 teaspoon salt	**1½ oz (40 g) blue cheese, crumbled**
1 rounded teaspoon mustard powder	**2 spring onions, finely chopped**
	freshly milled black pepper

Start off by crushing the garlic clove together with 1 teaspoon of salt down to a creamy mass in a pestle and mortar, then add the mustard and work that in. Next add the lemon juice, vinegar and after that the oil. Mix everything together thoroughly, then in a bowl combine the soured cream and mayonnaise and gradually whisk into the dressing ingredients. When all is thoroughly blended, add the chopped spring onions and the crumbled blue cheese. Season with freshly milled pepper. The dressing is now ready to use, and I think a few crunchy croûtons are a nice addition when you come to dress the salad (see page 28).

———————— ◊ ————————

Balsamic Vinaigrette Dressing

·

MAKES ENOUGH FOR A SALAD FOR 6 PEOPLE

Balsamic vinegar, which is now widely available, has done wonders for the modern cookery repertoire, imparting its rich, dark, distinctive flavour to very many dishes. In vinaigrette it really comes into its fullest glory.

1 tablespoon balsamic vinegar	**1 rounded teaspoon mustard powder**
4 tablespoons extra virgin olive oil	**1 level teaspoon Maldon salt**
1 fat clove garlic	**freshly milled black pepper**

A pestle and mortar is indispensable for making vinaigrette. All you do is peel a clove of garlic, pop it in the bowl along with the salt and smash the garlic with the pestle – as it breaks down and mingles with the salt, it will turn very quickly into a creamy mass. Now add the mustard and several good grinds of freshly milled pepper, and work these into the garlic. Next mix in first the vinegar and then the oil, and when everything's amalgamated pour the whole lot into a small screw-top jar until you're ready to serve the salad. Give it a hefty shake before using.

NOTE: Don't make vinaigrette too far in advance – it's best made not more than an hour or so before you need it.

———— ◊ ————

CHAPTER THREE

SUMMER FISH
and
SHELLFISH

———— ◊ ————

*I*t is a paradox that just as the decline in the number of high-street fishmongers is reaching alarming proportions, so fish is beginning to assume a more and more important role in the British diet. There is a growing number – not least among my own family and friends – of what I call 'semi-veggis': that is, people who won't eat meat but who *do* eat fish and are constantly calling for new ideas and recipes.

Happily the quality and variety of fish available in supermarkets has improved greatly in recent years, but there is still one deficiency that distresses me and that is the short supply of true wild salmon that migrates to the rivers from the sea where it has had the benefit of its traditional diet of crustaceans which give it its highly prized flavour. Young people are rarely excited by salmon simply because they have most often, if not always, tasted indifferent farmed fish rather than the real thing. It need not be so: I have tasted farmed salmon from Norway that was excellent, so there is hope.

Meanwhile my suggestion is to try once each summer to get hold of the real thing – expensive but worth it – and to use one of the several recipes in this chapter, all of which are expressly devised to keep in that glorious flavour while cooking.

————————————

Salmon Rösti Fish Cakes

·

SERVES 4 AS A MAIN COURSE OR 8 AS A STARTER

I've got a thing about fish cakes: if ever they appear on a restaurant menu I always order them – and I'm frequently trying to dream up new variations. This one is a real winner. You can make it with any fish: it doesn't have to be salmon. Serve them with Toasted Sweetcorn Salsa (page 50), which is a cross between a sauce and a salad, low in calories and absolutely delicious.

12 oz (350 g) tail end of salmon (ask the fishmonger to remove the skin and bones)	**2 tablespoons fresh lime juice**
	a couple of pinches of cayenne pepper
8 oz (225 g) firm-fleshed new potatoes (Cyprus are a good variety for this)	**salt**
	groundnut oil for frying
2 tablespoons chopped fresh coriander	
	TO GARNISH:
1 heaped tablespoon capers, drained and roughly chopped (or, if they're very small, left whole)	**sprigs of fresh coriander**

Begin by washing the potatoes, then place them in a saucepan (skins on), add salt and just cover with boiling water from the kettle. Put a lid on and boil for 10 minutes.

Meanwhile chop the salmon into chunks and give it a few pulses in a food processor to chop it fairly finely (or you can do this by hand). Now place the salmon in a mixing-bowl and add the capers, lime juice and chopped coriander leaves. Mix well and season with salt and cayenne. When the potatoes have had their 10 minutes they won't be cooked through, but that's how we want them. Drain them and, when they are cool enough to handle, peel off the skins and grate them using the coarse blade of a grater. Then carefully combine them with the salmon, trying not to break up the grated bits.

Now take tablespoons of the mixture and slap them into cakes: you need to press the mixture firmly together but don't worry about the ragged edges because these look pretty when they cook. Repeat until the mixture is used up: you should have twelve cakes. Measure 1–2 tablespoons of oil into a frying-pan and, when the oil is really hot, add the fish cakes. Fry them for 3 minutes on each side to a crusty golden colour. Drain on kitchen paper as they leave the pan, and serve garnished with sprigs of coriander and accompanied by Toasted Sweetcorn Salsa (see page 50).

———— ◊ ————

Rösti Crab Cakes

·

SERVES 2 AS MAIN COURSE OR 4 AS STARTER

*A*s a great lover of any type of fish cake I have always adored American crab cakes, but somehow the small English crabs seem too rich for them. After some serious tasting comparisons with my husband, scoring out of ten, the following recipe gets top marks. The potato counteracts the richness of the crab more effectively than the usual breadcrumbs, and served with Pickled Limes (page 202) you complete a marriage made in heaven!

8 oz (225 g) mixed prepared crabmeat	**1 heaped tablespoon chopped fresh**
5 oz (150 g) firm waxy potatoes	**coriander or parsley**
1 slightly rounded tablespoon capers,	**salt and freshly milled black pepper**
drained and chopped (or, if they're	**groundnut oil for frying**
very small, left whole)	
1 tablespoon fresh lime juice	
1 teaspoon grated lime zest	**TO GARNISH:**
2 spring onions, finely chopped	**sprigs of fresh coriander or flat-leaf**
(including the green parts)	**parsley**
2 pinches of cayenne pepper	**lime quarters**

First put the unpeeled potatoes in a saucepan with boiling water and salt, and simmer them for exactly 10 minutes. Meanwhile measure out the rest of the ingredients into a mixing bowl and mix together thoroughly. When the potatoes are cooked, drain them and as soon as they are cool enough to handle, peel off the skins and grate the flesh on the coarse blade of the grater, pushing the potatoes all the way down the length of the grater so that the strips are as long as possible.

Now carefully combine the grated potato with the crab mixture, trying not to break up the pieces of potato. Have a flat tray or baking-sheet handy, then take rough tablespoons of the mixture and form them into eight little cakes, squeezing and pressing them evenly together – don't worry about any ragged edges: this is precisely what gives the crab cakes their charm when cooked.

When the cakes are made, cover them with clingfilm and leave in the refrigerator for at least 2 hours to chill and become firm. To cook, heat 1½ tablespoons of oil in a frying-pan, making sure it is very hot, then gently slide in the crab cakes using a spatula. Cook them for 3 minutes on each side, turning the heat down to medium. Don't turn them over until the 3 minutes are up or they will not be firm enough. Remove them to a plate lined with kitchen paper, then transfer them to a warmed serving-plate and garnish with lime quarters and coriander or flat-leaf parsley. Serve with Pickled Limes (page 202) or with Toasted Sweetcorn Salsa (page 50) or Avocado Salsa (page 51).

Rösti Crab Cakes

Toasted Sweetcorn Salsa

.

SERVES 4

*I*f possible, make this salsa about half an hour before you serve it to allow the flavours to develop.

2 cobs sweetcorn, stripped of husks and threads	**2 tablespoons chopped fresh coriander**
½ red pepper, very finely chopped	**2 tablespoons fresh lime juice**
½ medium red onion, finely chopped	**a few drops of tabasco sauce**
2 large firm tomatoes, skinned, de-seeded and chopped	**salt and freshly milled black pepper**
	a little olive oil

First pre-heat the grill to its highest setting, then rub the corn kernels with a trace of olive oil. Place them under the grill and toast them for roughly 8 minutes, turning them from time to time so that they toast evenly. When they're cool enough to handle, hold each one firmly with a cloth and scrape off all the kernels using your sharpest knife. Then mix these together with all the other ingredients, taste to check the seasoning and serve with the Salmon Rösti Fish Cakes (page 47).

———————— ◊ ————————

Avocado Salsa

·

SERVES 4

This avocado salsa – a cross between a sauce and a salad – not only complements the flavour of salmon, but it also looks so pretty against the pink of the fish.

1 ripe but firm avocado	**2 tablespoons fresh lime juice**
2 large firm tomatoes	**a few drops of tabasco sauce**
½ small red onion	**salt and freshly milled black pepper**
1 rounded tablespoon chopped fresh coriander	

Skin the tomatoes by pouring boiling water over them, then leaving for exactly 1 minute before draining and slipping the skins off when they're cool enough to handle. Then cut each tomato in half and, holding each half over a saucer (cut side downwards), squeeze gently to extract the seeds. Now chop the tomato flesh as finely as possible.

Next halve the avocado, remove the stone, cut each half into quarters and peel off the skin. Chop the avocado into minutely small dice, and do the same with the onion. Finally combine everything together in a bowl, adding seasoning, the lime juice, chopped coriander and a few drops of tabasco. Cover with clingfilm and leave on one side for an hour before serving to allow the flavours to develop.

Serve this salsa with either grilled or baked salmon or the Salmon Rösti Fish Cakes (see page 47).

———————— ◊ ————————

Salmon *with a* Saffron Cous-cous Crust

·

SERVES 4

This is unusual but works like a dream and is very simple to prepare. The cous-cous crust encases the salmon and keeps all the fragrant juices inside intact. Served with the Tomato and Olive Vinaigrette (opposite) and perhaps some fresh shelled peas, it makes a perfect main course for summer entertaining.

4 × 5 oz (150 g) boned and skinned fillets of salmon
5 oz (150 g) medium cous-cous
7 fl oz (200 ml) dry white wine
2–3 good pinches of saffron stamens
1 egg, beaten
salt and freshly milled black pepper

You will also need a baking-sheet, lightly greased.

Pre-heat the oven to gas mark 5, 375°F (190°C).

First of all prepare the cous-cous – which is dead simple. All you do is place it in a bowl, then heat up the wine till just at simmering point, whisk the saffron into it along with some salt and pepper, and pour the whole lot over the cous-cous grains. Then leave the cous-cous on one side until it has absorbed all the liquid. After this fluff it by making cutting movements across and through it with a knife.

Now take each salmon fillet, season with salt and pepper, and dip it first into beaten egg, then sit it on top of the cous-cous and using your hands, coat it on all sides, pressing the cous-cous evenly all round (it works in just the same way as breadcrumbs). Now place the coated fillets on the baking-sheet and if you want, cover with clingfilm and keep refrigerated until they're needed. When you are ready to cook, pop them into the pre-heated oven and bake for 15–20 minutes or a little longer if the fish is very thick. Serve each one in a pool of Tomato and Olive Vinaigrette, and hand the rest of the vinaigrette separately.

———— ◊ ————

Tomato *and* Olive Vinaigrette

8 oz (225 g) tomatoes, skinned, de-seeded and chopped small	**1 tablespoon white wine vinegar**
3 oz (75 g) pitted black olives, chopped to the same size as the tomatoes	**1 teaspoon grain mustard**
1 fat clove garlic	**1 tablespoon chopped fresh chervil or flat-leaf parsley**
4 fl oz (110 ml) olive oil	**rock salt and freshly milled black pepper**
1 tablespoon lemon juice	

Crush the garlic with 1 teaspoon of rock salt, using a pestle and mortar, then add the mustard, vinegar, lemon juice, olive oil and a good seasoning of black pepper, and whisk thoroughly. About half an hour before serving add the tomatoes, olives and chopped chervil or flat-leaf parsley.

◊

Salmon Steaks *with* Avocado *and* Crème Fraîche Sauce

·

SERVES 6

If you want to serve something really special for a summer dinner party that leaves you utterly free from any hassle, this cold salmon dish fits the bill perfectly. Although this recipe serves six, you can in fact line up the salmon steaks in any number you like – twelve or even twenty-four – which makes it ideal for buffet parties and celebrations.

FOR THE SALMON:	1 small clove garlic, peeled
6 fresh salmon steaks, weighing approx. 6 oz (175 g) each	1 teaspoon sherry vinegar
6 small sprigs of fresh tarragon	salt and freshly milled black pepper
2 bayleaves	
6 dessertspoons white wine	TO GARNISH:
salt and freshly milled black pepper	1 bunch watercress or other pretty leaves
FOR THE SAUCE:	
1 good-sized avocado	Pre-heat the oven to gas mark 4, 350°F (180°C).
1 × 200-ml tub crème fraîche	

First of all take a large sheet of foil (approx. 36 × 24 inches/90 × 60 cm) and lay it in a shallow baking-tin. Wipe the pieces of salmon with kitchen paper and place each one on the foil. Now put a small sprig of tarragon on top of each one along with a piece of bayleaf (these ingredients are there simply to perfume the salmon very subtly without altering its flavour).

Now season with salt and freshly milled pepper and finally spoon a dessertspoon of wine over each salmon steak before wrapping the whole lot loosely in the foil. Make a pleat in the top to seal it. Place the foil parcel on a highish shelf in the oven for exactly 20 minutes. Then remove the tin from the oven and let the salmon cool inside the foil without opening it.

Meanwhile prepare the sauce. Halve the avocado, remove the stone, then divide into quarters and peel off the skin using a sharp knife if necessary. Place the flesh in a liquidiser or food processor then, using a teaspoon, scrape the avocado skin to remove the last greenest part and add that to the rest.

Now pop in the garlic clove, then measure in the sherry vinegar, add salt and pepper and blend until smooth. Next remove the purée to a mixing-bowl and simply fold in the crème fraîche till it's thoroughly blended. Taste to check the seasoning – it might need a spot more vinegar. Cover the bowl with clingfilm and keep in the refrigerator until you're ready to serve. This should be made only a few hours in advance to keep the luscious green colour at its best.

When you're ready to serve the salmon, undo the foil and, using a sharp knife, ease off the strip of skin around the edge of each steak and discard it. Remove the herbs, then transfer the fish to a serving-dish and decorate with small bunches of watercress or other leaves placed in the hollow centre. Hand round the sauce separately.

NOTE: If you prefer you can cook boned-out salmon fillets in exactly the same way, using 5 oz (150 g) fillets and cooking them for only 10–15 minutes.

———————— ◊ ————————

Hot *and* Sour Pickled Prawns

·

SERVES 4 AS A STARTER

*T*his is an ace of a first course for busy people. It is dead easy to prepare, and as it needs at least 48 hours to pickle the prawns and allow the flavours to develop, there's absolutely nothing to do at the last minute. You can, if you want, use ordinary-sized prawns (or even the ready-peeled frozen kind), but best of all are the fat, juicy and sweet Mediterranean prawns which are now available in most supermarkets in rigid plastic containers or else vacuum-packed. Please don't worry about there being a whole dessertspoon of tabasco in the marinade – it really doesn't make it fiery-hot, but gives it what I'd call a lively piquancy.

16 large cooked Mediterranean prawns	**1 dessertspoon Worcestershire sauce**
½ medium yellow pepper, very thinly sliced	**1 dessertspoon tabasco sauce**
½ medium red pepper, very thinly sliced	**½ level teaspoon salt**
	freshly ground black pepper
	1 level teaspoon white sugar
2 oz (50 g) red onion, thinly sliced	
½ lemon, thinly sliced	**TO GARNISH:**
1 tablespoon drained capers	**sprigs of coriander**
5 fl oz (150 ml) light olive oil	**½ lime, thinly sliced**
2 fl oz (55 ml) cider vinegar	
juice of 2 limes	**You will also need a 1½-pint (1-litre)**
1 level teaspoon mustard powder	**non-metallic dish or polythene box.**

To prepare the prawns, remove the shells and heads (if there are any) but leave the tails on as they look very attractive. Then use the tip of a small sharp knife to cut a slit all along the back of each prawn and remove the black thread that sometimes runs from head to tail. Then place the prawns and capers in the dish together with the sliced peppers, onion and lemon.

Now in a bowl or jar whisk the oil, mustard, vinegar, lime juice, Worcestershire sauce and tabasco together, adding salt, a little coarsely ground black pepper and 1 level teaspoon of sugar, then pour this mixture all over the prawns. Cover the container and place it in the refrigerator for at least 48 hours, giving the contents a shake or stirring them around from time to time.

Serve the prawns garnished with sprigs of coriander and slices of lime with plenty of the marinade poured over and lots of bread to mop up the juices.

———— ◊ ————

Hot and Sour Pickled Prawns

Fried Skate Wings *with* Warm Green Salsa

·

SERVES 2

Skate wings have everything going for them. They have a fine-flavoured, creamy flesh which comes away from the bone with no fuss or bother, and they're dead easy to cook. I love them shallow-fried to a crisp golden colour, with the following sharp, lemony and quite gutsy sauce poured in at the last moment. Serve with a mixture of dressed green salad leaves, and some tiny new potatoes.

FOR THE SKATE:	**1 heaped tablespoon capers, drained**
1 lb (450 g) skate wings (2 small or 1 large cut in half)	**1 heaped teaspoon grain mustard**
	1 medium clove garlic
1 heaped tablespoon seasoned flour	**1 tablespoon chopped fresh basil**
2 tablespoons oil	**2 tablespoons chopped fresh flat-leaf parsley**
	2 tablespoons fruity olive oil
FOR THE GREEN SALSA:	**4 tablespoons fresh lime juice**
4 anchovy fillets, drained and finely chopped	**½ teaspoon rock salt**
	freshly milled black pepper

I think it's preferable to make the sauce not too far ahead as the parsley tends to discolour, though you could make up most of the sauce in advance and add the parsley at the last moment – either way, it's very quick and easy. All you do is crush a clove of garlic with ½ teaspoon of salt using a pestle and mortar (or on a board using the back of a tablespoon) till you get a paste-like consistency. Then simply combine this with all the other sauce ingredients and mix everything very thoroughly.

To cook the skate wings, take a 10-inch (25-cm) frying-pan and put it on a gentle heat to warm up while you wipe the fish with kitchen paper and then coat it with a light dusting of seasoned flour. Now turn the heat up to high, add the oil to the pan and, as soon as it's really hot, add the skate wings.

Fry them for about 4–5 minutes on each side depending on their size and thickness – slide the tip of a sharp knife in and push to see if the flesh parts from the bone easily and looks creamy white. Then pour in the sauce all round the fish to heat very briefly. It doesn't need to cook but simply to warm a little. Serve the fish straight away with the sauce spooned over.

NOTE: This sauce works well with fried cod steaks or any other fried fish.

———————— ◊ ————————

Thai Red Curry Paste

·

MAKES 8 TABLESPOONS, ¹/₂ PINT (275 ML)

This dark, pungent curry paste makes a delightful alternative to dry, ground spices. I have included it in the prawn recipe on page 61, the fish cake recipe on page 60 and the chicken recipe on page 126, so it's best to make it in bulk, freeze and use it as and when you need it. It freezes really well, which means that you don't have to shop for small amounts of the ingredients – which may take some finding.

4 stems lemon grass, trimmed and chopped (see page 18)	6 cloves garlic
	4 level teaspoons coriander seeds
4 medium red chillies	2 level teaspoons cumin seeds
2 teaspoons grated fresh ginger	grated zest and juice of 2 limes
4 shallots	2 dessertspoons hot paprika

Begin by splitting the chillies in half and removing and discarding the seeds. After that wash your hands, because the seeds are very fiery and if you touch the delicate skin on your face after handling them it can smart and burn (I've done it so often!). Now take a small frying-pan and pre-heat it over a medium heat, then add the coriander and cumin seeds and toss them around in the dry pan to roast them and draw out their flavours. After about 5 minutes tip them into a mortar and crush them finely to a powder.

Now simply place the chillies, spices and all the other ingredients into a food processor and whizz them to a coarse paste. Then measure out the quantity you need for the fish cakes and freeze the rest in 2-tablespoon portions – and don't forget to label and date. It will keep for 2 months.

———— ◊ ————

Thai Fish Cakes
with Cucumber Dipping Sauce

·

SERVES 2 AS A MAIN COURSE OR 4 AS A STARTER

I*f you have some red curry paste to hand (see page 59), these little fish cakes make a wonderfully different first course, especially if the rest of the meal has a spicy theme.*

1 lb (450 g) any white fish (cod, haddock, hake, etc.), weighed after boning and skinning, then cut into chunks	**FOR THE CUCUMBER DIPPING SAUCE:**
	2 inches (5 cm) unpeeled cucumber
	2 shallots or salad onions
	1 small carrot
2 spring onions, very finely sliced into rounds (including the green parts)	**1 small green chilli, de-seeded**
	1 teaspoon grated fresh ginger
	1 tablespoon roasted peanuts
2 tablespoons fresh coriander leaves	**1 tablespoon soft brown sugar**
2 heaped tablespoons Thai Red Curry Paste (see page 59)	**4 fl oz (110 ml) rice vinegar or wine vinegar**
1 tablespoon fresh lime juice	**1 tablespoon light soy sauce**
salt	**1 tablespoon groundnut oil**
1 green chilli, de-seeded	
2 tablespoons groundnut oil for frying	**TO GARNISH:**
	sprigs of fresh coriander

Simply place the chunks of fish, the coriander leaves, lime juice, spring onions, curry paste, chilli and a little salt in a food processor and blend till you have a finely minced texture – don't blend it to a fine purée, though, as this is not so good. Transfer to a mixing-bowl. Next take dessertspoons of the mixture and form them into balls, squeezing the mixture together. Then place them on a flat surface and flatten them out with the palm of your hand into small cake shapes about 1½ inches (4 cm) in diameter. You should get 16 in all. When all the fish cakes are ready, put them on to a plate, cover with clingfilm and leave them in the refrigerator for a couple of hours to firm up.

Meanwhile, make the sauce. Place the cucumber, shallots or salad onions, carrot, chilli, ginger and peanuts in the goblet of a food processor and whizz till very finely chopped. Transfer the chopped vegetables to a bowl. Next mix the sugar with the vinegar to dissolve it, then pour it over the vegetables along with the soy sauce and groundnut oil. Mix thoroughly.

To cook the fish cakes, heat 2 tablespoons of groundnut oil in a frying-pan and, when it's very hot and beginning to shimmer, fry the cakes for about 1 minute on each side, then drain on crumpled kitchen paper. Garnish with sprigs of coriander and serve with the cucumber dipping sauce.

———— ◊ ————

Angel-hair Pasta
with Thai Spiced Prawns

·

SERVES 2 AS A MAIN COURSE OR 4 AS A STARTER

Angel-hair pasta (capellini) is, as the name suggests, the very finest shreds of pasta, now available in larger supermarkets. Large prawns also come in packs, peeled with the tails intact: the very large varieties come in eight per pack, the smaller ones in twelve per pack. Either way you need one pack per person as a main course. The recipe is spicy, pungent and just the thing to make use of some previously prepared Thai curry paste (see page 59).

6 oz (175 g) angel-hair pasta	grated zest and juice of 1 lime
2 packs prawns (see above)	salt and freshly milled black pepper
4 slightly rounded tablespoons Thai Red Curry Paste (see page 59)	
5 cloves garlic, chopped	TO GARNISH:
2 large tomatoes, skinned, de-seeded and chopped	3 tablespoons chopped fresh coriander
2 tablespoons light olive oil	a few paper-thin slices of fresh lime,
7 fl oz (200 ml) dry white wine	cut in half

A couple of hours before you intend to serve the pasta, place the Thai Red Curry Paste in a bowl, add the prawns and toss them around so that they get a good coating of sauce. Now cover the bowl with clingfilm and leave in the fridge for a couple of hours for the prawns to soak up the flavours.

When you're ready to start cooking, first heat up 2 tablespoons of oil in a frying-pan and gently cook the garlic for 1 or 2 minutes or until it's pale gold, then add the chopped tomatoes, lime zest and juice and wine and keeping the heat high, let the sauce bubble and reduce for about 8 minutes. After that add the prawns and paste to the sauce and when it's bubbling again, turn the heat down and let it cook gently for another 3 minutes or until it has reduced and thickened. Then put a lid on the pan and keep the sauce warm while you deal with the pasta.

For this you need to make sure that you have two serving-plates warming, then bring a large saucepan of salted water up to a fast boil. Push the pasta down into the boiling water and immediately time it for 3 minutes only. As soon as the 3 minutes are up, spoon the pasta (using a spoon and fork, or a proper pasta server) directly on to the plates. Don't worry about the wetness as this will soon evaporate: if you drain this pasta in the normal way, because it's so fine it sticks together and becomes unmanageable. Now quickly spoon the sauce and prawns over the pasta, sprinkle on the coriander, add the lime slices and serve *presto pronto*!

◊

Thai Salmon Filo Parcels

·

SERVES 2

For waist-watchers and the health-conscious the growing popularity of filo pastry is, I'm sure, warmly welcomed. But I also suspect we could be in danger of overkill, so I like to use it only where it's really appropriate – like here, where a parcel of something really does seal in all those precious salmon juices, and when they mingle with the lime, ginger and coriander the result is marvellous!

2 salmon fillets cut from the thicker part of the fish, weighing 4–5 oz (110–150g) each	**1 oz (25 g) butter**
	salt and freshly milled black pepper
4 sheets filo pastry, each approx. 12 × 7 inches (30 × 18 cm)	**TO GARNISH:**
1 teaspoon grated fresh ginger	**sprigs of coriander**
grated zest and juice of 1 lime	**1 lime, cut into quarters**
1 clove garlic, crushed	
1 tablespoon chopped fresh coriander	**You will also need a baking-sheet.**
1 small spring onion, finely sliced	Pre-heat the oven to gas mark 5, 375°F (190°C).

First of all, in a small bowl mix together the ginger, lime zest, garlic, coriander and spring onion, then stir in the lime juice. Now melt the butter in a small saucepan, then lay 1 sheet of filo pastry out on a flat surface, brush it all over with melted butter, spread another sheet of filo on top and brush this lightly with melted butter as well.

Now position one of the salmon fillets near to one end of the filo, season it and sprinkle half the lime and herb mixture on top. Next fold the short end of pastry over the salmon, then fold the long sides inwards, fold the salmon over twice more and trim any surplus pastry (it's important not to end up with great wedges of pastry at each end). Wrap the other piece of salmon in exactly the same way and, when you're ready to cook, brush the parcels all over with melted butter, place them on the baking-sheet and bake in the oven for 20–25 minutes or until the pastry is brown and crisp. Serve garnished with sprigs of coriander and wedges of lime to squeeze over.

———— ◊ ————

Baked Salmon *and* Sorrel Creams

·

SERVES 6 AS A STARTER

The sharp, almost lemony flavour of sorrel leaves contrasts beautifully with fresh salmon. Supermarkets sell them now, but if they're not available young spinach leaves or even outer lettuce leaves can be used instead. The leaves are used to make a kind of casing around the salmon, which looks very pretty.

6 oz (175 g) fillet of salmon (prepared weight)	**salt and freshly milled black pepper**
2 oz (50 g) young sorrel or spinach leaves, de-stalked and washed	
8 fl oz (225 ml) milk	**TO GARNISH:**
5 fl oz (150 ml) double cream	**watercress**
2 level teaspoons chopped fresh tarragon	**You will also need 6 × 4 fl oz (110 ml) ramekins, lightly buttered, and a baking-sheet.**
4 × large egg yolks	
1 bayleaf	Pre-heat the oven to gas mark 3,
1 blade of mace	325°F (170°C).

First steam the sorrel leaves for 1 minute only using a fan steamer. Pat them dry and line the ramekins with them. You'll probably find a pastry brush is helpful here to ease the leaves into place. Overlap them so as not to leave any gaps, and allow the tops to hang over the dish edges as they can be folded in afterwards.

Now to deal with the fish, place it in a saucepan along with the milk, bayleaf and blade of mace, add some salt and pepper, then bring it up to simmering point and simmer for 4 minutes exactly – no more, as it needs to be really moist. Strain the milk into a jug, then flake the salmon into large flakes and divide them equally among the ramekins, sprinkling in the chopped tarragon and a little seasoning.

Return the milk to the saucepan, add the cream and heat gently while you whisk the egg yolks in the jug the milk was in. As soon as the milk mixture barely simmers, pour it over the eggs, whisk again thoroughly, then pour the whole lot into the ramekins. Fold any overlapping leaves over the mixture, then transfer them on the baking-sheet to a highish shelf of the oven to bake for 20–25 minutes or until the centres of the creams are just set and the tops turning brown. Remove them from the oven and leave them for 10–15 minutes to settle before turning them out on to warmed serving-dishes. Garnish with watercress and serve straight away. These also taste good served with some young salad leaves dressed with Lemon Vinaigrette (see page 76).

◊

Chilled Marinated Trout
with Fennel

.

SERVES 2

*T*his makes a very appropriate main course for a warm day. It's a doddle to prepare and it has the advantage of being cooked and left to marinate, so that when the time comes you have literally nothing to do but serve it. We like this either with a plain mixed-leaf salad or with a half-quantity of Pesto Rice Salad (see page 36).

2 × 8 oz (225g) bright fresh rainbow trout	**1 tablespoon lemon juice**
1 lb (450 g) ripe red tomatoes, skinned and chopped	**½ teaspoon fresh oregano**
	salt and freshly milled black pepper
1 bulb fennel, trimmed and sliced (green tops reserved)	
8 fl oz (225 ml) dry white wine	**FOR THE GARNISH:**
1 clove garlic, finely chopped	**2 small spring onions, finely chopped**
1 small onion, finely chopped	**2 tablespoons chopped parsley**
¾ teaspoon whole black peppercorns	**grated zest of 1 lemon**
¾ teaspoon coriander seeds	**fennel tops**
½ teaspoon fennel seeds	
2 tablespoons extra virgin olive oil	**You will also need a 10-inch (25-cm) frying-pan or wide shallow pan.**
1 tablespoon white wine vinegar	

Begin by washing the fish and drying it with kitchen paper. Then warm the frying-pan over a gentle heat, crush the peppercorns, coriander and fennel seeds in a mortar, add the crushed spices and let them dry-roast for about 1 minute to draw out the flavours. Then add the olive oil, garlic and onion and let them cook gently for about 5 minutes or until the onion is pale gold.

Next add the tomatoes, lemon juice, wine vinegar and white wine, stir and, when it begins to bubble, season with salt and pepper and add the oregano. Now add the sliced fennel to the pan, followed by the trout, basting the fish with the juices. Put a timer on and give the whole thing 10 minutes' gentle simmering. After that use a fish slice and fork to turn each fish over carefully on to its other side – don't prod it or anything like that or the flesh will break. Then give it another 10 minutes' cooking on the other side.

After that gently remove the trout to a shallow serving-dish, spoon the sauce all over, cool, cover with clingfilm and leave them in a cool place. If you want to make this dish the day before, that's OK provided you keep it refrigerated and remove it an hour before serving. Either way sprinkle each trout with the garnish (made by simply combining all the ingredients together) before taking to the table.

NOTE: If the weather's chilly, this dish is excellent served warm with tiny new potatoes and a leafy salad.

———————— ◇ ————————

Californian Grilled Fish

.

SERVES 2

If you have a jar of the lovely coriander and lime tartare sauce (see page 67), a wonderful way to use it is to spread it on to some fish fillets, then sprinkle with cheese and breadcrumbs and pop them under a pre-heated grill. You'll have one of the fastest and most delectable suppers imaginable.

2 fish fillets (cod, hake, whiting, plaice, sole – anything you like), weighing approx. 7 oz (200 g) each

2 tablespoons Quick Coriander and Lime Tartare Sauce (see page 67)

grated zest of ½ lime

3 tablespoons grated Cheddar cheese

2 tablespoons white or brown breadcrumbs

1 dessertspoon chopped fresh coriander

pinch of cayenne pepper

½ oz (10g) butter

salt and freshly milled black pepper

You will also need a grill pan lined with foil smeared with a trace of butter.

Pre-heat the grill to its highest setting.

Begin by wiping the fish fillets with kitchen paper to get them as dry as possible, then place them in the foil-lined grill pan. Season with salt and pepper, then spread the tartare sauce all over the surfaces of the fish. Now in a bowl mix the breadcrumbs, cheese, coriander, cayenne and lime zest together, then sprinkle this over the fish as evenly as possible. Dot with a little butter. Place the grill pan as far from the heat as possible and grill the fish for 10–15 minutes depending on its thickness – it should be just cooked through and the top should be crispy and golden. Serve with tiny new potatoes tossed in chives and lemon juice, and a plain lettuce salad.

———————— ◊ ————————

Quick Coriander *and* Lime Tartare Sauce

·

SERVES 4

When someone brought me back a menu from the famous Bel Air Hotel in Los Angeles and I saw this sauce, I couldn't wait to try it. I love the way American chefs are unafraid to introduce eastern ingredients into western recipes – in this case a classic tartare sauce normally made with lemon juice and parsley is transformed by the more oriental flavours of lime juice and coriander. Brilliant.

1 large egg	3 large or 4 small cornichons (continental gherkins), finely chopped
6 fl oz (170 ml) light olive oil	
1 small clove garlic, peeled	1 tablespoon chopped fresh coriander
1 dessertspoon fresh lime juice	½ teaspoon mustard powder
1 heaped tablespoon small capers, drained	½ teaspoon salt
	freshly milled black pepper

Tartare sauce has a mayonnaise base, which in this case is made by the quick method: that is, using a whole egg and a food processor or blender. Break the egg into the bowl of the processor, add salt, pepper, garlic and mustard powder, then switch on the motor and, through the feeding tube, add the oil in a thin, steady trickle, pouring it as slowly as you can (which even then will take only about 2 minutes). When the oil is in and the sauce has thickened, transfer it to a bowl using a rubber spatula, then add all the other ingredients. Taste to check the seasoning before serving. This sauce will keep in a screw-top jar in the refrigerator for up to a week. Serve with any plain grilled fish or with fish cakes.

———— ◊ ————

THE VEGETABLES
of
SPRING *and*
SUMMER

———— ◊ ————

During the summer in which I was preparing this book a disconcerting thing happened. Included in my once-a-week supermarket shopping was a bag containing fresh young peas in the pod; the checkout girl (who looked all of sixteen) puzzled over the bag, trying, I thought, to find the price. But then she looked up and said, 'Can you tell me what these are, please?' How sad that any young person would not have had the pleasure of bursting open moist young pods and munching on the odd raw tender pea – for me it was always one of the lazy pleasures of summer, sitting in the garden shelling peas. What happened, of course, is that the frozen market took over and only those peas too old for freezing found their way on sale as 'fresh', which made people *think* they didn't like fresh peas – and the same applies to young broad beans. I do hope that English growers won't entirely abandon the fresh market, so that we can all still enjoy them.

This chapter does not contain many recipes as such, but that is because of my conviction that young vegetables do not need recipes: it would be almost criminal to mask their flavour in any way. Later on in summer, though, they might need a little help from the cook and that is why the idea of oven-roasting them has fired my imagination. There are a number of suggestions on this way of cooking in the book, and I can assure you that it adds a whole new dimension to the vegetables and, as a bonus, they require very little attention while cooking.

————————

Warm Potato Salad
with Lemon *and* Chive Vinaigrette

·

SERVES 4–6

This recipe can be served warm, as an accompanying vegetable, or cold as part of a group of salads – in which case you still need to pour on the dressing while the potatoes are warm.

2 lb (900 g) new potatoes (as small as possible), skins on, washed	**1 heaped teaspoon grain mustard**
2 sprigs of fresh mint	**1 clove garlic**
salt	**1 teaspoon rock salt**
	freshly milled black pepper

FOR THE LEMON AND CHIVE VINAIGRETTE:	
4 tablespoons lemon juice	**TO GARNISH:**
grated zest of 1 lemon	**2 tablespoons snipped fresh chives**
4 tablespoons extra virgin olive oil	**6 spring onions, trimmed and chopped small**

First of all place the potatoes in a saucepan with enough boiling water just to cover them, add the mint and some salt, and simmer them for about 15–20 minutes.

Meanwhile make the vinaigrette. Using a pestle and mortar, crush the garlic and salt together to a paste, then gradually whisk in all the other dressing ingredients.

When the potatoes are cooked, drain them in a colander and transfer them to a serving-bowl. Pour on the vinaigrette dressing while they are still hot, toss them around in the dressing to get a good coating, then finally scatter in the chopped chives and spring onions and serve.

———————— ◊ ————————

Oven-roasted Ratatouille

·

SERVES 4

If you like ratatouille, once you've tried it roasted like this you'll never go back to the traditional method. Not only do the vegetables retain their shape and identity, but they also take on a lovely toasted flavour.

1 lb (450 g) cherry tomatoes, skinned	**3 tablespoons olive oil**
2 medium courgettes	**1 handful fresh basil leaves**
1 small aubergine	**salt and freshly milled black pepper**
1 small red pepper, de-seeded and cut into 1-inch (2.5-cm) squares	
1 small yellow pepper, de-seeded and cut into 1-inch (2.5-cm) squares	**You will also need a large shallow roasting-tin approx. 16 × 12 inches (40 × 30 cm) (see page 194).**
2 fat cloves garlic, finely chopped	
1 medium onion, peeled and chopped into 1-inch (2.5 cm) squares	Pre-heat the oven to its highest setting.

Prepare the courgettes and aubergine ahead of time by cutting them into 1-inch (2.5-cm) dice, leaving the skins on. Now sprinkle with 1 dessertspoon salt, then pack them into a colander with a plate on top and a heavy weight on top of that. Leave them like this for an hour so that the bitter juices can drain out. After that squeeze out any juices that are left and dry the vegetables thoroughly in a clean cloth.

Now arrange the tomatoes, aubergine, courgettes, peppers and onion in a roasting-tin and sprinkle the garlic over them. Roughly tear up the basil leaves and mix with the olive oil. Drizzle the oil over the vegetables, making sure that each one has a good coating, and finally season with salt and pepper. Roast on the highest shelf of the oven for 30–40 minutes or until the vegetables are roasted and tinged brown at the edges. Remove from the oven using an oven glove as the tin will be very hot and serve straight away.

———————— ◊ ————————

Sliced Potatoes Baked *with* Tomatoes *and* Basil

·

SERVES 4–6

*J*ust *when the new potatoes are getting too big to be really new, the red ripe tomatoes of summer are at their best and the basil leaves are large and opulent. This dish is a wonderful way to combine all three. We love to serve this with the Chicken with Sherry Vinegar (page 128).*

2 lb (900 g) potatoes, skins on
1 lb (450 g) red ripe tomatoes
3 tablespoons fresh basil leaves
1 onion, finely chopped
1 fat clove garlic, finely chopped
1 tablespoon extra virgin olive oil
salt and freshly milled black pepper

You will also need a round or oval gratin dish approx. 9 inches (23 cm) wide, lightly oiled.

Pre-heat the oven to gas mark 5, 375°F (190°C).

First of all pour boiling water over the tomatoes, leave them for 1 minute, then drain them and slip the skins off, protecting your hands with a cloth as necessary. Chop the flesh quite small. Then slice the potatoes thinly. Now, in a gratin dish, arrange first a layer of sliced potato, a little chopped garlic and onion and some seasoning followed by some chopped tomato, some more seasoning and a few torn basil leaves. Repeat all this until you have incorporated all the ingredients, then drizzle a little oil over the surface and bake in the oven for about 1 hour or until the potatoes are tender.

———————— ◊ ————————

Roasted Fennel Niçoise

·

SERVES 4 AS A STARTER

The slight aniseed flavour of fennel holds its own perfectly with the gutsy provençale flavours of anchovies, olives and tomatoes. This is a lovely dish to serve warm with fish, meat or poultry, or on its own as a starter, or even cold as a salad as part of a buffet lunch.

3 medium bulbs fennel	**2 tablespoons lemon juice**
1 tablespoon olive oil	**5 tablespoons extra virgin olive oil**
	1 teaspoon rock salt
FOR THE DRESSING:	**freshly milled black pepper**
2 large continental-type tomatoes, skinned, de-seeded and finely chopped	**TO GARNISH:** **a few fresh basil leaves and fennel fronds**
12 black olives, pitted and chopped	
1 clove garlic	**You will also need a shallow roasting-tray.**
1 shallot, finely chopped	
4 anchovy fillets, drained and chopped	Pre-heat the oven to gas mark 5, 375°F (190°C).

Begin by preparing the fennel. First trim off any green fronds and reserve them for the garnish. Now lay the fennel bulbs flat on a board and trim off the root base, then cut the stalk ends away by making two diagonal cuts so that the bulbs look pointed at the top. Cut each one first into quarters, cut away the centre stalky parts, then slice the quarters into eighths – but be careful to leave the layers attached to the root ends.

Now place the fennel in a saucepan, pour boiling water over, season with some salt and simmer for just 5 minutes, no longer. Then drain the fennel in a colander so it can dry off a little. Next put 1 tablespoon olive oil in a saucer and use it to brush the roasting-tray and each piece of fennel before arranging them on the tray. Roast the fennel on a high shelf in the oven for 30 minutes or until it is nicely tinged with brown at the edges and is cooked through but still retains some bite.

While the fennel is roasting, make up the dressing. In a pestle and mortar crush the garlic to a paste together with 1 teaspoon of salt, then whisk in the lemon juice and oil, and, when it is amalgamated, combine it with the rest of the ingredients.

When the fennel's ready, transfer it to a shallow serving-bowl and pour the dressing over it while it is still warm. Taste to check the seasoning – it will need some freshly milled pepper – and scatter with the chopped fennel fronds and some torn basil leaves just before serving.

Compote of Garlic *and* Sweet Peppers

·

SERVES 6–8

This is a really robust, deliciously full-bodied combination that goes well with spicy sausages or barbecued meats. Serve as part of a buffet, and just see how many people go back for seconds!

2 lb (900 g) peppers (red, yellow and orange – but not green)	2 teaspoons mild chilli powder
3 tablespoons olive oil	10 cloves garlic, finely chopped
2 rounded teaspoons cumin seeds, lightly crushed	5 level tablespoons tomato purée
	salt

Begin by washing, halving and de-seeding the peppers, and cut the halves into quarters and the quarters into ¼-inch- (5-mm)-thick strips. Then place a large saucepan over a medium heat, add the crushed cumin seeds and toss them around in the heat to draw out their flavour. Then add the oil and let it gently heat for a minute. Now stir in the sliced peppers, garlic and chilli powder, cook for 1 minute, stirring so that the ingredients are thoroughly mixed, cover the pan and continue to cook over a low heat for a further 30–40 minutes or until the pepper strips are quite soft.

Now uncover the pan, increase the heat to medium and stir in the tomato purée. Continue to cook (uncovered) until no free liquid remains – this takes about 15 minutes. Finally taste and add salt and a little more tomato purée if the mixture seems to need a little more body and sweetness. Serve the compote warm, or if you want to serve it as part of a buffet it's fine served cool (but not chilled).

———————— ◊ ————————

Baby Summer Vegetables *with* Lemon Vinaigrette

·

SERVES 6–8

*T*his is another versatile recipe that can be served either warm as a vegetable or cold as a salad – a truly beautiful combination of those first, young, tender vegetables of early summer.

12 oz (350 g) broad beans (prepared weight) – about 4 lb (1.8 kg) in shell	**grated zest of 1 lemon**
8 oz (225 g) fresh tiny baby carrots	**2 tablespoons white wine vinegar**
8 oz (225 g) fresh garden peas – prepared weight (1½ lb (700 g) in shell)	**8 tablespoons light olive oil**
10 bulbous spring onions	**2 level teaspoons mustard powder**
	TO GARNISH:
FOR THE LEMON VINAIGRETTE:	**1 tablespoon chopped fresh herbs (mint and chives)**
3 tablespoons lemon juice	**You will also need a steamer.**

To get the very best colour and texture (and if you have the patience) it's best to fillet the broad beans. So after shelling pour boiling water over them and, when the water has cooled sufficiently, simply slip off the outer skin, which will reveal the beautiful vivid green inner bean in two halves. As you skin them, place them in a bowl.

Next put the carrots in a steamer fitted over a pan of simmering water, steam them for 4 minutes precisely, then add the spring onion bulbs and the peas and continue to steam for a further 3–4 minutes.

Meanwhile make up the vinaigrette dressing by placing all the ingredients together in a screw-top jar, putting on the lid and shaking vigorously to combine everything.

When the vegetables are tender but still retain their bite, remove the steamer, throw out the water from the pan and put the broad beans in the pan along with the rest of the vegetables and the dressing and toss everything around over a gentle heat for about 1 minute. Then transfer it all to a warmed serving-dish, sprinkle the herbs over as a garnish and serve.

———————— ◊ ————————

Baby Summer Vegetables with Lemon Vinaigrette

Oven-roasted Potatoes *with* Garlic *and* Rosemary

·

SERVES 4–6

In keeping with the principle that outdoor eating needs to be gutsy, these little potatoes are just that. They're easy too – they don't need any attention; you just leave them in the oven till you're ready to serve.

2 lb (900 g) unpeeled large new potatoes, skins on

2 tablespoons fresh rosemary leaves, finely chopped

1–2 cloves garlic, finely chopped

2 tablespoons olive oil

salt and freshly milled black pepper

You will also need a shallow, solid roasting-tin measuring approx. 16 × 12 inches (40 × 30 cm).

Pre-heat the oven to gas mark 7, 425°F (220°C).

Begin by measuring the oil into the roasting-tin, then pop it into the oven to heat through. Wash the potatoes but don't scrape the skins off, then cut them into cubes of roughly ½ inch (1 cm). Place them in a clean tea-cloth and dry them as thoroughly as you can, then transfer them to a large plate.

Remove the tin from the oven, place it over direct heat – the oil needs to be very hot – then carefully slide the potatoes straight into the hot oil. Turn them around to get a good coating of oil, sprinkling in the garlic and rosemary as you go. Return the tin to the oven and roast for 30–40 minutes or until the potatoes are golden-brown and crisp. Season with salt and pepper before serving.

———— ◊ ————

Red-coated Courgettes

·

SERVES 2–4

The courgettes in our garden proliferate so quickly that I'm always looking for fresh ways of serving them. This is one of the most delicious and speediest.

12 oz (350 g) young courgettes	**1 heaped teaspoon fresh oregano**
12 oz (350 g) red ripe tomatoes	**2 tablespoons olive oil**
1 small onion, finely chopped	**salt and freshly milled black**
1 fat clove garlic, crushed	**pepper**

You will need your largest, widest frying-pan for this. Begin by heating 1 tablespoon of oil in the pan and frying the onion gently for 5 minutes. Meanwhile wipe the courgettes, trim off the ends and then cut them into slices about 1/4 inch (5 mm) thick. Now remove the onion to a plate. Turn the heat right up, add the second tablespoon of oil and, when it's really hot, add the courgette slices to the pan, spreading them out in one layer. Fry them to colour lightly on both sides.

While that's happening pour boiling water over the tomatoes, then after 1 minute slip the skins off and roughly chop the flesh. When the courgettes are coloured, return the onion to the pan and pour the chopped tomatoes over. Sprinkle in the crushed garlic, oregano and some seasoning and simmer gently, stirring every now and then, for about 10 minutes or until the tomato pulp has reduced and thickened and completely coats the courgettes.

◊

CHAPTER FIVE

BARBECUE *and* OUTDOOR FOOD

———— ◊ ————

I do feel we're beginning to catch up with the Australians and Americans in this sphere. Barbecuing won't ever become a way of life here, if only because of the weather, but you're more than likely to find a barbecue as a permanent fixture in someone's garden nowadays – not just for parties but often for everyday cooking.

In a way this type of cooking doesn't need recipes: plain steaks, sausages or chops all taste better cooked out of doors on charcoal. So do certain fish like fresh silvery herring, mackerel and sardines – and have you ever tried kippers on the barbecue? In Suffolk we get wonderful local-smoked kippers, and they taste their absolute best brushed with oil and cooked over charcoal. The reason they fit the bill for outdoor eating so well is that they have a strong gutsy flavour. Somehow subtle flavours get lost in the open air, so the whole point of the recipes in this chapter is that they have lots of character and flavour. What pleases me most is that at last I've found a barbecue recipe for vegetarians (page 90), who are the ones who so often feel left out of this type of meal.

The kind of barbecue you use is a matter of personal choice, but I do commend to you the self-lighting charcoal that comes in small bags which are placed on the tray complete. All you do is light the bag: the coals burn evenly, are ready for cooking in 20–30 minutes and there's no fuss or mess.

————

Preceding page from left to right: Crispy salad with American Blue Cheese Dressing (page 42); All-American Half-pounders (page 86); Oven-roasted Potatoes with Garlic and Rosemary (page 78).

A Mixed Grill
with Apricot Barbecue Glaze

·

SERVES 6

This is a sauce that's suitable for all meats — lamb cutlets, pork ribs or chicken drumsticks. The quantity is enough to glaze six of each, which makes a nice mixture of meats to serve to six people. One important point is that drumsticks need pre-baking in a pre-heated oven at gas mark 4, 350°F (180°C), for 15 minutes just before glazing and barbecuing.

6 small to medium chicken drumsticks	**2 fl oz (55 ml) Worcestershire sauce**
6 lamb cutlets	**2 fl oz (55 ml) light soy sauce**
6 pork ribs	**1 tablespoon grated fresh ginger**
	1 rounded teaspoon ginger powder
FOR THE APRICOT BARBECUE GLAZE:	**a few drops of tabasco sauce**
2 large apricots	**2 tablespoons tomato purée**
2 rounded tablespoons dark brown sugar	**1 clove garlic**
	freshly milled black pepper

Begin by placing the apricots in a small saucepan with enough water to cover them, then bring them up to simmering point and simmer for 2 minutes. Now drain off the water and, as soon as they are cool enough to handle, slip off the skins. Then halve and stone them and place the flesh in a blender or food processor together with all the other glaze ingredients. Whizz everything to a purée and the sauce is ready.

All you need to do now is arrange the lamb and pork in a shallow dish, pour the glaze over them — turning the pieces of meat so that each one gets a good coating — then cover and leave in a cool place until you're ready to cook.

When you light the charcoal pre-cook the chicken drumsticks as above then, when your charcoal is at the right heat, brush the drumsticks with the glaze and cook for about 5 minutes on each side about 3 inches (7.5 cm) from the coals. The ribs and cutlets will need about 6 minutes on each side, but take the lamb off before 12 minutes if you like it very rare.

What we like to do sometimes is scrape any sauce that's left in the dish into a small saucepan, add a glass of white wine to it and bring it all up to simmering point to give some extra sauce. Serve the barbecued glazed meats with Oven-roasted Potatoes with Garlic and Rosemary (page 78), a crisp salad and some very robust red wine!

——————— ◊ ———————

Spiced Lamb *and* Cashew Kebabs

•

SERVES 4

Not long ago I was fortunate enough to have a holiday in Hong Kong and visited a restaurant at Repulse Bay called Spices. I was so taken by the spicy kebabs I had there that on my return home I immediately tried to make them – and I think this is fairly close to the original!

12 oz (350 g) neck fillet of lamb (80 per cent lean meat, as some fat is important to keep it juicy)	**juice of ½ lime**
	1 fresh green chilli, de-seeded
1 small onion, quartered	**a little groundnut oil**
1 clove garlic	**1 level teaspoon cumin seeds**
4 oz (110 g) roasted and salted cashew nuts	**1 level teaspoon coriander seeds**
	salt and freshly milled black pepper
3 tablespoons chopped fresh coriander leaves	**You will also need 4 long, flat metal skewers.**

First of all you need to roast the spices, and to do this place them in a small frying-pan or saucepan over a medium heat and stir and toss them around for about 1–2 minutes or until they begin to look toasted and start to 'jump' in the pan. Now transfer them to a pestle and mortar and crush them to a powder.

To make the kebabs you need to cut the meat into chunks and place it in a food processor along with the onion, garlic, fresh coriander leaves, lime juice, cashews, spices and seasoning. Now switch the motor on and off until you have ground everything together but it still has some identity – it needs to end up like very coarse sausagemeat. Now take about a tablespoon of the mixture (don't forget to remove the blade first!) and roll it on a flat surface into a sausage shape, squeezing the mixture firmly together. Pat and square off the ends to give a nice shape. Repeat until you have used all the mixture: you should aim to finish up with twelve. Thread these on to skewers, three on each. Cover them with clingfilm and keep them in the fridge until you need them (it's important to leave them for at least 2 hours anyway to firm up).

Before grilling brush the kebabs with oil and cook for about 5 minutes on each side either indoors, 2 inches (5 cm) from the grill, or outside over hot charcoal. Serve with Sweet Pepper and Coriander Relish (page 85) and some Spiced Pilau Rice (page 124).

◊

Sweet Pepper *and* Coriander Relish

.

SERVES 4

This is made in moments if you have a food processor, and you won't believe how good it tastes. Serve it with Spiced Lamb and Cashew Kebabs (page 84) or with plain grilled or barbecued meats.

1 fresh green chilli	**4 tablespoons fresh lime juice**
1 medium red pepper	**2 large tomatoes, skinned,**
1 small red onion	**de-seeded and chopped**
4 tablespoons chopped fresh coriander	**salt and freshly milled black pepper**

Just place all the ingredients in a food processor and switch on to blend evenly to the stage where it looks as though everything has been chopped minutely small but hasn't lost its identity. Leave on one side (covered) in a cool place, and stir well before serving.

———————— ◊ ————————

All-American Half-pounders

·

SERVES 4

There are several kinds of hamburgers, ranging from those that come frozen or served up in fast-food chains to the slightly more classy supermarket varieties. Few people, I suspect, have tasted the real thing which consists of good steak chopped and tenderised, formed into burgers and grilled on charcoal. The degree of thickness is paramount, since that ensures a crisp, charred outside and a juicy, rare, medium-rare or whatever-you-like inside. I find that 4 oz (110 g) of meat is perfect if it is going to be served in a bun, but 8 oz (225 g) is best for a more sophisticated adult version. Personally I prefer it to eating a plain grilled steak.

2 lb (900 g) best beef (rump if you're feeling flush, otherwise chuck or blade steak; either way, make sure that it contains 20 per cent fat)	**salt and freshly milled black pepper**
	a little oil

If you're on a diet, don't eat a hamburger: it really is vital that it contains 20 per cent fat, as this is what keeps the meat moist while cooking. If you're using chuck steak, trim off any gristle and sinewy bits but hang on to the fat. Cut the meat into chunks, put it into a food processor and blend until it looks like fine minced beef; however, don't overdo the processing, because if the meat becomes too fine, the burger will have a bouncy texture!

Empty the meat into a bowl and season with freshly milled pepper, but don't add salt till after the cooking because it draws out the juices. Now form the mixture into four rounds, pressing each one firmly together (it won't need egg or anything else to keep it together if you press firmly enough). Now place the burgers on a plate, cover with clingfilm and leave in the refrigerator until you're ready to cook them.

When the barbecue is good and hot, brush the grill with a little oil to prevent the meat sticking to it, and give the burgers a light coating of oil too. Grill them for 4–6 minutes on each side, depending on how you like them. The same timing also applies to a domestic grill turned to its highest setting.

Serve the half-pounders with Mexican Tomato Salsa (page 87), Oven-roasted Potatoes with Garlic and Rosemary (page 78) or, if you like, a blue cheese salad (see page 42).

NOTE: If you do not have a food processor, pass the steak through the fine blade of a mincer.

Mexican Tomato Salsa

·

SERVES 4

*S*alsa has the advantage of being a salad, sauce and relish all in one. There's no fat or sugar in it, and the flavour's wonderful. The small, squat, green chillies are not too hot, so if you'd like a little more kick to this you can add a few drops of tabasco.

4 large firm tomatoes	**1 fresh green chilli (the fat squat**
½ medium red onion, finely chopped	**variety that isn't too fiery)**
2 heaped tablespoons chopped fresh	**juice of 1 lime**
coriander	**salt and freshly milled black pepper**

Place the tomatoes in a bowl, pour boiling water over them, then after 1 minute drain them and slip off the skins, protecting your hands with a cloth if you need to. Now cut each tomato in half and hold each half in the palm of your hand (cut side up), then turn your hand over and squeeze gently until the seeds come out – it's best to do this over a plate or bowl to catch the seeds!

Now, using a sharp knife, chop the tomatoes into approximately ¼-inch (5-mm) dice straight into a serving-bowl. Next de-stalk the chilli, cut it in half, remove the seeds and chop the flesh very finely before adding it to the tomatoes. Add the chopped onion, coriander and lime juice, and season with salt and pepper. Give everything a thorough mixing, then cover and leave on one side for about an hour before serving.

———— ◊ ————

Barbecued Sardines *with* Summer Herb Sauce

·

SERVES 4

*S*ardines have a very evocative flavour and aroma that perfectly suit eating out of doors. This is a recipe that can easily be prepared well ahead of time, and if the coals on the barbecue are good and hot the fish are cooked in moments. If sorrel is unavailable use young spinach leaves mixed with some grated zest of lemon – about 1 tablespoon – for the stuffing.

2 lb (900 g) fresh sardines (approx. 12)	2 teaspoons balsamic vinegar
6 oz (175 g) fresh sorrel leaves (stalks removed), washed and dried	1 rounded tablespoon snipped fresh chives
approx. 2 tablespoons olive oil	1 level tablespoon chopped fresh tarragon
salt and freshly milled black pepper	1 rounded tablespoon chopped fresh basil
FOR THE SAUCE:	1 rounded tablespoon chopped fresh flat-leaf parsley or chervil
3 shallots, finely chopped	
1 large clove garlic, finely chopped	salt and freshly milled black pepper
3 tablespoons cider vinegar	

First prepare the sardines. Use a small pair of scissors to cut open the bellies and remove the innards. Then wipe them inside and out with damp kitchen paper and arrange them on a plate. Next chop the sorrel leaves fairly finely, then season and use three-quarters of them to stuff inside the bellies of the fish. Sprinkle the oil over the fish and rub it in so that they all get a good coating.

Now prepare the sauce by placing the remaining sorrel leaves along with the other herbs, the shallots and garlic in a jug or serving-bowl and add 5 tablespoons boiling water followed by the vinegars. Stir well and season with salt and pepper.

The sardines will need very little time to cook – just 2 minutes on each side. Serve with the sauce handed round separately. These are also very good served with Oven-roasted Potatoes with Garlic and Rosemary (page 78) and Roasted Fennel Niçoise (page 74).

NOTE: If it rains, the sardines will cook perfectly well under a domestic grill or on a ridged grill pan.

———— ◊ ————

Barbecued Sardines with Summer Herb Sauce

Marinated Halloumi Cheese Kebabs
with Herbs

·

SERVES 2

Vegetarians often tend to feel deprived when invited to barbecues, so we spent an entire day last summer finding something that grills well on charcoal and has all the fun and flavour – but without meat. This was the one that fitted the bill perfectly.

12 oz (350 g) halloumi cheese, cut into 1-inch (2.5-cm) cubes	**1 level teaspoon each of chopped fresh thyme, oregano, rosemary, mint and parsley (or similar combination of whatever herbs are available)**
1 medium pepper (any colour)	
1 medium red onion	
4 medium cap mushrooms	**juice of 1 lime**
	freshly milled black pepper

FOR THE MARINADE:

2 fl oz (55 ml) extra virgin olive oil

1 fat clove garlic

You will also need 2 × 12-inch (30-cm) flat metal skewers.

Begin by cutting the pepper and onion into even-sized pieces about 1 inch (2.5 cm) square, to match the size of the cubes of cheese. Then chop the herbs and garlic quite finely and combine them with the oil, lime juice and some freshly milled pepper. Now place the cheese, onion, pepper and mushrooms in a large, roomy bowl and pour the marinade over them, mixing very thoroughly. Cover and place in the fridge for 24 hours, and try to give them a stir round every now and then.

When you're ready to barbecue the kebabs, take the two skewers and thread a mushroom on first (pushing it right down) followed by a piece of onion, a piece of pepper and a cube of cheese. Repeat this with more onion, pepper and cheese, finishing with a mushroom at the end. Place the kebabs over the hot coals, turning frequently till they are tinged brown at the edges – about 10 minutes. Brush on any left-over marinade juices as you turn them. Serve with Mexican Tomato Salsa (page 87) and Oven-roasted Potatoes with Garlic and Rosemary (page 78).

———————— ◊ ————————

Barbecued Sweetcorn

·

SERVES 4

I *think this is the nicest way to eat sweetcorn. Even if you don't have a barbecue going, you can still cook it under a pre-heated grill.*

2 cobs sweetcorn	**salt and freshly milled black pepper**
1 dessertspoon olive oil	

Remove the husks and threads from the sweetcorn, then brush the kernels all over with the oil, seasoning them liberally with salt and pepper as you go. Place the corns on the grill over hot coals and watch them carefully, turning them around with tongs so that all the kernels get toasted to a golden-brown colour. The whole process will take about 5–10 minutes, depending on how far the corn is from the heat – test each one with a skewer to check that it is tender. To serve, take your sharpest knife and cut the corns across into chunks. These are best eaten using your hands and just taking bites: delicious!

—————————— ◊ ——————————

Crunchy Peanut-coated Drumsticks

·

SERVES 6

Yes, it's really true. Even if you don't like peanuts in the 'normal' way, you'll enjoy them as a coating with a slightly oriental flavour – I've tested this on peanut haters! It is perfect picnic food for both children and adults, but remember to start these off at least 8 hours ahead.

12 chicken drumsticks, skin removed	**4 tablespoons milk**
5 tablespoons groundnut oil	**pinch of cayenne pepper**
2 tablespoons fresh lemon juice	**salt and freshly milled black pepper**
4 oz (110 g) plain flour	
2 level tablespoons medium curry powder	
6 oz (175 g) salted peanuts	**You will also need a very shallow**
2 tablespoons fresh coriander leaves	**baking-tin approx. 12 × 10 inches**
2 eggs, beaten	**(30 × 25 cm): large enough to hold the chicken in one layer.**

First of all lay the drumsticks in a dish, mix 2 tablespoons of the oil and the lemon juice together and pour this over the chicken. Then leave the drumsticks to marinate overnight or for at least 8 hours, turning them over once or twice during this period. To make the coating, mix the flour, curry powder and seasoning together in another shallow dish. When you are ready to cook, toss the drumsticks in the flour mixture, a few at a time, until well coated on all sides, tap off the surplus flour and lay them on a plate (reserve any unused flour). Pre-heat the oven to gas mark 7, 425°F (220°C).

Now place the nuts, coriander leaves, 2 tablespoons of the reserved flour and the cayenne in a food processor and blend till you have a mixture chopped minutely small, then transfer this to a plate. After that beat the eggs and milk together in a bowl. Then take each drumstick and dip it once more into the remaining seasoned flour, then into the egg mixture and finally into the peanut mixture. Return the coated drumsticks to their plate and keep cool till needed.

To cook, place the baking-tin containing the remaining 3 tablespoons of oil in the oven to pre-heat, then add the drumsticks to the hot oil (not allowing them to touch each other), baste well and bake on a high shelf for 15 minutes. Turn the drumsticks over, give them another 15 minutes, then pour off the oil and give them 5 more minutes to get really crisp. Drain on kitchen paper and when they are cold wrap them individually in foil for transportation.

———————— ◊ ————————

Oven-baked Chicken *with* Garlic *and* Parmesan

·

SERVES 4

This is excellent picnic food. Small chicken joints are so easy to transport and *have the advantage of being easy to eat without knives and forks when you get there.*

1 × 3½ lb (1.75 kg) chicken, cut into 8 joints (see the *Complete Illustrated Cookery Course* for instructions on jointing), or a mixture of 8 thigh and leg portions	1½ oz (40 g) Parmesan cheese, grated
	2 oz (50 g) butter
	4 tablespoons olive oil
	rock salt and freshly milled black pepper
4 large cloves garlic	
3 × medium eggs	
2 heaped tablespoons finely chopped fresh parsley	You will also need a shallow roasting-tin large enough to hold the chicken in one layer.
2 oz (50 g) fresh breadcrumbs	

First of all arrange the chicken joints in a shallow dish large enough to hold them in a single layer. Then place the garlic cloves in a mortar with 1 heaped teaspoon rock salt and crush the garlic to a purée. Now add this to the eggs, season with some pepper and whisk well with a fork before pouring the whole lot over the chicken joints. Cover the dish with clingfilm and leave in a cool place or the fridge for at least 4 hours, turning the chicken joints over half-way through.

Pre-heat the oven to gas mark 4, 350°F (180°C), and pop in the shallow roasting-tin containing the butter and oil to pre-heat as well. Meanwhile combine the breadcrumbs with the Parmesan, parsley and a little seasoning together on a plate, and spread out some absorbent kitchen paper on a flat surface. Remove the chicken from the fridge, take one piece at a time and carefully sit it in the crumb mixture, patting and coating it all over with crumbs (trying not to disturb the egg and garlic already clinging to it). Then lay each piece as it's coated on the kitchen paper. Next remove the tin with the now-hot fat in it from the oven and add the chicken pieces, baste them well and bake on a high shelf for 20 minutes. Then turn the chicken pieces over and give them another 20 minutes, before finally pouring off the excess fat from the tin and giving them another 5 minutes.

Drain them on more kitchen paper, leave to cool and wrap the pieces individually in foil for transportation.

NOTE: This is also excellent served hot at home with some sliced, lightly sautéed bananas as a garnish.

———— ◊ ————

Home-made Lemonade

·

MAKES 3 PINTS (1.75 LITRES)

There really isn't anything quite like it. There are a million and one commercial versions, but nothing can compare with the flavour of fresh lemons made into lemonade.

6 large lemons	**approx. 5 oz (150 g) granulated sugar**

First scrub the lemons in warm water, then thinly pare the coloured outer zest from 3 of them using a potato peeler or zester. After that any white pith will need to be pared from the strips of zest with a sharp knife – this is important to prevent the lemonade tasting bitter. Now put the zest in a large bowl and add the squeezed juice of all the lemons (don't bother to strain the juice at this stage) and the sugar.

Next pour in $2^{1}/_{2}$ pints (1.4 litres) of boiling water, then stir well, cover and leave overnight in a cool place. Next day stir again and taste to check the sweetness, adding a little more sugar if it needs it. Now strain through a fairly coarse sieve, as it's nice if some of the lemon remains. Pour it into bottles, using sterilised corks, then chill thoroughly. Serve the lemonade either straight or diluted with soda water, with lots of ice.

NOTE: To make lemon barley water proceed as above but in addition take 4 oz (110 g) of pearl barley and rinse thoroughly under a cold tap. Place it in a saucepan and cover with 2 inches (5 cm) of cold water. Then bring it to the boil and simmer for 3–4 minutes. After that drain it through a sieve and then rinse and drain it again before combining it with the lemon juice, zest, sugar and boiling water. Leave in a cool place for 24 hours. Then strain and bottle as above.

——————— ◊ ———————

Pineapple Cooler

·

SERVES 6–8

This is a most extraordinary drink. It sounds so unlikely, but it really does taste good – not like pineapple but more like cider. It's very refreshing on a hot summer's day, and it's great fun to make in that it uses only the skin of the pineapple which is normally thrown away – so there's nothing to lose!

the rind of 1 ripe medium	sprigs of fresh mint
pineapple, well rinsed	ice
approx. 2 oz (50 g) caster sugar	

First of all cut the stalky top and the base off the pineapple and discard these. Now stand the pineapple upright on its base and, using a sharp knife, cut away the skin in long strips, working your way all round the fruit. Reserve the fruit itself for a dessert.

Now get to work with a sharp knife, chopping the skin into small pieces about 1 inch (2.5 cm) square. Then pile them all into a bowl, pour over 1½ pints (850 ml) cold water, then cover the bowl with a cloth and leave at room temperature for 3–4 days or until the mixture is bubbly and fermenting. Strain it into a jug, add sugar to taste and serve with lots of ice and sprigs of mint.

———————— ◊ ————————

Debbie Owen's
Iced Tea

·

SERVES 6–8

The British may be experts at making and serving tea, but when it comes to iced tea the Americans have the edge. It must be the most refreshing drink to serve when the weather is hot and humid. I first tasted this version at my friends' the Owens' Fourth of July party several years ago and have been addicted to it ever since. It's like a non-alcoholic Pimms, so it's perfect for serving to drivers.

6 English Breakfast tea-bags	**½ orange, sliced**
10 fl oz (275 ml) freshly squeezed orange juice, chilled	**½ lemon, sliced**
juice of ½ lime	**2 level tablespoons caster sugar**
approx. 12 sprigs of fresh mint	**lots of ice**

Make up some very strong tea in a large teapot using the tea-bags and 2 pints (1.2 litres) boiling water. Then add 2 tablespoons of sugar and 6 sprigs of mint to the teapot. Allow the tea to infuse for 15–20 minutes, then remove the tea-bags and leave it to get absolutely cold. When the tea is cold remove the mint from the teapot. After that put lots of ice into a glass jug and pour in the cold tea followed by the orange and lime juices and 6 more sprigs of mint. Finally add the orange and lemon slices, stir thoroughly, and serve in glasses with more ice.

Summer Entertaining

Below are a few suggested menus for a variety of summer entertaining.

A SUPPER PARTY FOR 8 PEOPLE

First course
Mixed-leaf Caesar Salad (recipe × 2)

Sun-dried Tomato and Ricotta Bread Rolls

Main course
Baked Leg of Lamb with Rosemary with Redcurrant and Mint Sauce

Sliced Potatoes Baked with Tomatoes and Basil (recipe × 1½)

Fresh shelled peas

Dessert
Fromage Frais Cheesecake with Strawberry Sauce

——————— ◊ ———————

A VEGETARIAN SUPPER PARTY FOR 4 PEOPLE

First course
Chilled Lemon Grass and Coriander Vichyssoise

Mini Focaccias

Main course
Roasted Vegetable Cous-cous Salad with Harissa-style Dressing

Dessert
Vanilla Cream Terrine with Raspberries and Blackcurrant Coulis

——————— ◊ ———————

A Fourth of July American Barbecue for 8 People

First course
Salad of Cos and Webb's lettuce and rocket with American Blue Cheese Dressing (recipe × 2) and Parmesan croûtons (page 28)

Main course
All-American Half-pounders (recipe × 2)

Mexican Tomato Salsa (recipe × 2)

Oven-roasted Potatoes with Garlic and Rosemary (recipe × 2)

Home-barbecued Sweetcorn

Dessert
Hot Fudge Sundaes (make double of everything for those inevitable seconds – anything left over can be kept for a rainy day)

———————— ◊ ————————

A Quick and Easy Supper for 4 Busy People

First course
Fresh Asparagus with Foaming Hollandaise

Main course
Chicken Basque

Mixed-leaf Salad with Balsamic Vinaigrette Dressing

Dessert
Summer Fruit Compote with crème fraîche

———————— ◊ ————————

A Summer Buffet Party for 18 People
(including vegetarian choices)

First course
Roasted Tomato Salad (recipe × 2)

Hot and Sour Pickled Prawns (recipe × 2)

Compote of Garlic and Sweet Peppers

Main course
Salmon Steaks with Avocado and Crème Fraîche Sauce

Oven-baked Chicken with Garlic and Parmesan

Savoury Fetta Cheesecake with Preserved Pickled Peaches

Pesto Rice Salad (recipe × 3)

Roasted Fennel Niçoise (recipe × 3)

Baby Summer Vegetables with Lemon Vinaigrette (recipe × 3)

Green Peppercorn Bread Rolls (recipe × 1½)

Wholegrain Bread with Sunflower and Poppy Seeds (recipe × 1½)

Dessert
Summer Fruit Terrine (make 2)

Caramel Meringues with Mascarpone Cream (recipe × 2)

Fresh Peaches Baked in Marsala with Mascarpone Cream

———————— ◊ ————————
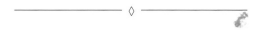

CHAPTER SIX

A VEGETARIAN SUMMER

———— ◊ ————

Time was when a vegetarian was just that: someone who ate no meat or fish, but only vegetable products. Nowadays there are many shades of opinion and many layers of being a non-meat eater. Throughout this book – not just in this chapter – I have included all kinds of recipes that do not contain meat, but there are also quite a number for those who are pure vegetarians. Hence this particular section, though by inclination I would prefer not to isolate it as something apart. In my last television series I said, 'I don't believe in vegetarian cooking,' and was taken to task by a number of people. In fact it was an unfortunate edit, for I went on to say (or would have done if it had not been cut) that vegetarian cooking now belonged in the mainstream of cookery and not as something 'special'.

Although I eat meat and fish, I do believe that we all owe much to the vegetarian movement – not least for persuading us to make better use of a wider range of vegetables, pulses and so on. The challenge now, which I'm delighted to see many restaurants and manufacturers beginning to take up, is to make vegetarian recipes even more imaginative and special.

————————————

Rigatoni *and* Asparagus *au* Gratin

·

SERVES 2

*T*his is an excellent way to turn 8 oz of asparagus stalks into a substantial supper dish for two people.

5 oz (150 g) rigatoni	**¾ oz (20 g) butter**
8 oz (225 g) asparagus (prepared weight)	**a grating of fresh nutmeg**
	salt and freshly milled black pepper
1½ tablespoons extra virgin olive oil	
1½ oz (40 g) Pecorino cheese, pared into shavings with a potato peeler	**You will also need an ovenproof gratin dish 7 × 7 inches × 2 inches deep (18 × 18 cm × 5 cm deep), lightly buttered.**
1½ oz (40 g) Parmesan cheese, finely grated	
1 lb (450 g) ripe red tomatoes, skinned and chopped	
10 fl oz (275 ml) milk	Pre-heat the oven to gas mark 6, 400°F (200°C).
¾ oz (20 g) plain flour	

First of all place the milk, flour and butter in a saucepan and whisk together over a gentle heat until the sauce begins to simmer and thicken. Then season with salt and pepper and a good grating of nutmeg. After that turn the heat down to its lowest setting and let the sauce cook for 3 minutes, then stir in the grated Parmesan, remove from the heat, cover with a lid and leave on one side while you prepare the other ingredients.

Prepare the asparagus by cutting the stalks diagonally into pieces roughly the same size as the rigatoni. Then take a 9-inch (23-cm) frying-pan, heat up the oil in it and sauté the asparagus pieces for about 5 minutes, tossing them around the pan and keeping the heat fairly high so that they colour at the edges. Then add the tomatoes to the pan, and let them bubble and reduce for about 1 minute. Then turn the heat off.

Next cook the pasta in plenty of boiling salted water (to which a few drops of oil have been added) for 6 minutes only; then drain it in a colander. Return it to the saucepan, add the sauce and the asparagus mixture and mix thoroughly. Taste to check the seasoning, pour the whole lot into the gratin dish, sprinkle with the shavings of Pecorino cheese and bake in the oven for 8–10 minutes. Serve straight away.

———————— ◊ ————————

Savoury Fetta Cheesecake

·

SERVES 6–8

The idea of a savoury cheesecake is for me quite new. In the testing we've had several misses, mainly because they somehow tasted too cheesy. This one, however, is a real winner. Fetta cheese lightened with fromage frais makes a lovely cool summer cheesecake, just right for a light lunch served with a salad, and a really wonderful accompaniment would be the Preserved Pickled Peaches on page 200.

FOR THE BASE:

3 oz (75 g) white breadcrumbs

1½ oz (40 g) Pecorino Romano cheese, finely grated (if not available, you can use Parmesan)

1 oz (25 g) butter, melted

freshly milled black pepper

FOR THE FILLING:

8 oz (225 g) fetta cheese

8 oz (225 g) medium-fat curd cheese

6 oz (175 g) fromage frais (8 per cent fat content)

2 level teaspoons gelatine powder or a vegetarian equivalent

2 teaspoons fresh lemon juice

1 tablespoon water

4 heaped tablespoons chopped fresh chives

3 spring onions, finely sliced

2 egg whites

freshly milled black pepper

You will also need an 8-inch (20-cm) round cake tin with a loose base. If it is less than 2 inches (5 cm) deep, line the sides with silicone baking parchment to give a depth of 2 inches (5 cm).

Pre-heat the oven to gas mark 6, 400°F (200°C).

Begin by putting the breadcrumbs in a bowl and adding the cheese, the melted butter and a seasoning of pepper (no salt because the cheese is quite salty). Now press the crumb mixture into the base of the prepared tin, pressing it firmly flat with the back of a spatula. Then pop it into the oven on a high shelf and bake for 15 minutes or until it is crisp and toasted golden-brown. Then remove from the oven.

Now for the filling: measure the lemon juice and water into a small tea-cup, sprinkle in the gelatine and leave on one side for 10 minutes to allow the gelatine to soak into the liquid. Then place the cup in a small saucepan containing a little water and allow it to simmer gently until the gelatine is completely liquid and has turned transparent. Leave the cup in the warm water so that it doesn't set.

Meanwhile make the filling by first breaking up the fetta cheese with a fork and then adding this to a food processor along with the curd cheese and fromage frais and blend until completely smooth. Then transfer to a bowl and stir in the chives, spring onions and some freshly milled pepper. Next, in a separate clean bowl, whisk the egg whites to the soft-peak stage.

Now you must act fairly quickly – pour the gelatine through a strainer on to the cheese and stir to combine it thoroughly, then follow this with the whisked egg whites, first folding 1 tablespoon of the whites into the cheese mixture to loosen it, then stirring in the remaining whites. Pour the whole lot on to the cooled base, cover with clingfilm and transfer the cheesecake to the fridge to chill and set until needed.

———————— ◊ ————————

Twice-baked Goat's Cheese
Soufflés *with* Chives

·

*I*s there anyone who doesn't love to eat a fluffy cheese soufflé straight from the oven? But, oh, the anxiety for the cook who has to commute to the kitchen to keep peering into the oven – and then finds that the guests all want to go to the bathroom the moment the soufflé gets to the table! Well, now you can relax, because twice-cooked soufflés can be made 2 or 3 days in advance (or even weeks if you want to freeze them). All you then do is turn them out on to a baking-sheet and bake them 25 minutes before you need them. They are extremely well-behaved when cooked and, although they may lose some of their puffiness if kept waiting, we have eaten them half an hour after cooking and they still taste great.

8 fl oz (225 ml) milk	**TO SERVE:**
1 small onion, cut in half	**freshly grated Parmesan cheese**
1 oz (25 g) unsalted butter	
1 oz (25 g) self-raising flour	
4 oz (110 g) peppered goat's cheese, cut into ¼-inch (5-mm) cubes	**You will also need 4 × 5 oz (150 ml) ramekins, 3 inches (7.5 cm) across and**
2 × medium eggs, separated	**1½ inches (4 cm) deep, well buttered,**
1 dessertspoon snipped fresh chives	**a roasting-tin and a solid**
1 bayleaf	**baking-sheet.**
a grating of fresh nutmeg	
a few whole black peppercorns	Pre-heat the oven to gas mark 4,
salt and freshly milled black pepper	350°F (180°C).

Begin by placing the milk, onion, bayleaf, a good grating of nutmeg, a few whole peppercorns and some salt in a small saucepan. Slowly bring it up to simmering point, then strain it into a jug and discard the onion, bayleaf and peppercorns. Now rinse and dry the saucepan, place it back on the heat and melt the butter in it. Stir in the flour and cook gently for 1 minute, stirring all the time, to make a smooth, glossy paste. Now add the hot milk little by little, stirring well after each addition. When all the milk is incorporated, let the sauce barely bubble and thicken, then leave it on the lowest possible heat for 2 minutes.

Now take the sauce off the heat and transfer it to a large mixing-bowl. Beat in first the egg yolks followed by the snipped chives. Mix everything thoroughly together and taste to check the seasoning. Finally fold in three-quarters of the cubed goat's cheese.

Next, the egg whites should go into another clean bowl and be whisked up to the soft-peak stage. Then take a heaped tablespoon at a time and fold the egg whites into the cheese-and-egg mixture using cutting and folding movements so as not to lose the air. Now divide the mixture between the buttered ramekins, place them in the roasting-tin and pour about ½ inch (1 cm) of boiling water straight from the kettle into the tin.

Place the roasting-tin on a high shelf in the oven and bake the soufflés for 15 minutes or until they are set and feel springy in the centre (it is important not to under-cook them at this stage, because on the second cooking they are going to be turned out). Don't worry if they rise up a lot – as they cool they will sink back into the dish. Remove them from the roasting-tin straight away, then cool and chill in the fridge until needed (they can also be frozen at this stage).

To serve the soufflés, pre-heat the oven to gas mark 6, 400°F (200°C). Butter a solid baking-sheet, then slide the point of a small knife round each soufflé, turn it out on to the palm of your hand and place it the right way up on the baking-sheet, keeping it well apart from its neighbours. Sprinkle the remaining goat's cheese on top of each one, then pop them into the oven on the middle shelf and bake for 20–25 minutes or until they're puffy, well-risen and golden-brown.

Using a fish slice, slide each soufflé on to a hot serving-plate and serve straight away with some freshly grated Parmesan sprinkled over. Serve on a salad of rocket leaves dressed with Balsamic Vinaigrette (page 43) to which you have added 1 oz (50 g) chopped sun-dried tomatoes.

NOTE: If you don't like goat's cheese use 4 oz (110 g) strong cheddar instead. Also, if you wish, you can give the soufflés their second cooking in the dishes without turning them out. But I think it's more fun to turn them out, and that way you get nice crusty edges.

———————— ◊ ————————

Roasted Vegetable Cous-cous Salad
with Harissa-style Dressing

·

SERVES 4 AS A MAIN COURSE OR 8 AS A STARTER

This salad is one of the best vegetarian dishes I've ever served. The combination of goat's cheese and roasted vegetables on a cool bed of cous-cous mixed with salad leaves and a spicy dressing is positively five-star.

1 quantity roasted vegetables (see page 110), with 1 small bulb fennel, chopped, substituted for the yellow pepper

FOR THE COUS-COUS:
10 oz (275 g) medium cous-cous
18 fl oz (500 ml) vegetable stock
4 oz (110 g) firm goat's cheese
salt and freshly milled black pepper

FOR THE SALAD:
1 × 3 oz (75 g) packet mixed salad leaves (such as lettuce, coriander leaves, flat-leaf parsley, rocket)

FOR THE DRESSING:
4 fl oz (110 ml) extra virgin olive oil
1 rounded teaspoon cayenne pepper
2 tablespoons ground cumin
2 heaped tablespoons tomato purée
4 tablespoons lime juice (approx. 2 limes)

TO GARNISH:
1 tablespoon black onion seeds

First prepare the roasted vegetables as on page 110, then remove them to a plate to cool. When you're ready to assemble the salad, first place the cous-cous in a large, heatproof bowl, then pour the boiling stock over it, add some salt and pepper, stir it with a fork, then leave on one side for 5 minutes, by which time it will have absorbed all the stock and softened.

Meanwhile cut the cheese into sugar-cube-sized pieces. Make up the dressing by whisking all the ingredients together in a bowl, then pour into a serving-jug. To serve the salad, place the cous-cous in a large, wide salad bowl and gently fork in the cubes of cheese along with the roasted vegetables. Next arrange the salad leaves on top and, just before serving, drizzle a little of the dressing over the top followed by a sprinkling of onion seeds and hand the rest of the dressing around separately.

———— ◊ ————

Roasted Vegetable Cous-cous Salad with Harissa-style Dressing

Roasted Mediterranean Vegetable Lasagne

·

SERVES 4–6

*B*aked lasagne is the most practical of dishes – it can be prepared well in advance and needs no more than a shove in the direction of the oven at the appropriate time. But sadly, because of over-exposure, the classic version is no longer the treat it used to be. This recipe follows the basic principles but incorporates the newer, smokier flavours of roasted Mediterranean vegetables. Even if you make it on a dull day, its dazzling colours will still be sunny.

approx. 9 sheets spinach lasagne (the kind that needs no pre-cooking)

FOR THE FILLING:
1 lb (450 g) cherry tomatoes, skinned
1 small aubergine
2 medium courgettes
1 small red pepper, de-seeded and cut into 1-inch (2.5-cm) squares
1 small yellow pepper, de-seeded and cut into 1-inch (2.5-cm) squares
1 large onion, sliced and cut into 1-inch (2.5-cm) squares
2 fat cloves garlic, crushed
3 tablespoons extra virgin olive oil
2 oz (50 g) pitted black olives, chopped
1 heaped tablespoon capers, drained
2 tablespoons fresh basil, leaves torn so that they stay quite visible
3 oz (75 g) mozzarella cheese, grated
salt and freshly milled black pepper

FOR THE SAUCE:
1¼ oz (35 g) plain flour
1½ (40 g) butter
1 pint (570 ml) milk
1 bayleaf
a grating of fresh nutmeg
salt and freshly milled black pepper
3 tablespoons grated Reggio Parmesan cheese

FOR THE TOPPING:
1 tablespoon grated Reggio Parmesan cheese

You will also need a large, shallow roasting-tin (or rimmed oven shelf) and a heatproof baking-dish measuring 9 × 9 inches × 2 inches deep (23 × 23 cm × 5 cm deep).

Pre-heat the oven to gas mark 9, 475°F (240°C).

Prepare the aubergine and courgettes ahead of time by cutting them into 1-inch (2.5-cm) dice, leaving the skins on. Then toss the dice in about a level dessertspoon of salt and pack them into a colander with a plate on top and a heavy weight on top of the plate. Leave them on one side for an hour so that some of the bitter juices drain out. After that squeeze out any juices left, and dry the dice thoroughly in a clean cloth.

Now arrange the tomatoes, aubergine, courgettes, peppers and onion in the roasting-tin, sprinkle with the chopped garlic, basil and olive oil, toss everything around in the oil to get a good coating, and season with salt and pepper. Now place the tin on the highest shelf of the oven for 30–40 minutes or until the vegetables are toasted brown at the edges.

Meanwhile make the sauce by placing all the ingredients (except the cheese) in a small saucepan and whisking continuously over a medium heat until the sauce boils and thickens. Then turn the heat down to its lowest and let the sauce cook for 2 minutes. Now add the grated Parmesan. When the vegetables are done, remove them from the oven and stir in the chopped olives and the capers. Turn the oven down to gas mark 4, 350°F (180°C).

Now, into the baking-dish pour one quarter of the sauce, followed by one third of the vegetable mixture. Then sprinkle in a third of the mozzarella and follow this with a single layer of lasagne sheets. Repeat this process, ending up with a final layer of sauce and a good sprinkling of grated Parmesan. Now place the dish in the oven and bake for 25–30 minutes or until the top is crusty and golden. All this needs is a plain lettuce salad with a lemony dressing as an accompaniment.

Pasta 'Puttanesca' (Tart's Spaghetti)

·

SERVES 2

In Italian a puttanesca *is a 'lady of the night', which is why at home we always refer to this recipe as tart's spaghetti. Presumably the sauce has adopted this name because it's hot, strong and gutsy – anyway, eating it is a highly pleasurable experience. If you are a strict vegetarian, replace the anchovies with another heaped tablespoon of capers.*

8–10 oz (225–275 g) spaghetti (depending on how hungry you are)	1 heaped tablespoon capers, drained
a few drops of olive oil	1 lb (450 g) tomatoes, skinned and chopped
salt	1 rounded tablespoon tomato purée
	1 dessertspoon chopped fresh basil
FOR THE SAUCE:	2 tablespoons extra virgin olive oil
2 cloves garlic, finely chopped	salt and freshly milled black pepper
2 oz (50 g) anchovies, drained	
6 oz (175 g) pitted black olives, chopped	TO GARNISH:
1 fresh red chilli, de-seeded and chopped	chopped fresh basil
	lots of freshly grated Parmesan cheese

To make the sauce, heat the oil in a medium saucepan, then add the garlic, chilli and basil and cook these briefly till the garlic is pale gold. Then add all the other sauce ingredients, stir and season with a little pepper – but no salt yet because of the anchovies.

Turn the heat to low and let the sauce simmer very gently without a lid for 40 minutes, by which time it will have reduced to a lovely thick mass, with very little liquid left.

While the sauce is cooking, take your largest saucepan, fill it with at least 4 pints (2.25 litres) of hot water and bring it up to a gentle simmer. Add a few drops of olive oil and a little salt and then, 8 minutes before the sauce is ready, plunge the spaghetti into the water. Stir well to prevent it clogging together, then time it for exactly 8 minutes.

After that drain it in a colander, return it to the saucepan *presto pronto*, and toss the sauce in it, adding the basil. Mix thoroughly and serve in well-heated bowls, with lots of grated Parmesan to sprinkle over – and have plenty of gutsy, 'tarty' Italian red wine to wash it down.

◊

Pasta 'Puttanesca'

Frijolemole

·

SERVES 4–6

This rather exotic title simply means 'bean purée' – but a rather special one, made with chickpeas, chillies, fresh lime juice and coriander. It has a crunchy texture and is lovely for a first course or light lunch with some toasted bread and a salad.

6 oz (175 g) dried chickpeas, soaked overnight in 1 pint (570 ml) cold water	**1 heaped tablespoon chopped fresh coriander**
1 tablespoon groundnut oil	**2 tablespoons soured cream or fromage frais**
1 medium Spanish onion, chopped	**salt and freshly milled black pepper**
2 cloves garlic, chopped	
3 spring onions	**TO GARNISH:**
1 fresh chilli	**black olives**
2 tablespoons fresh lime juice	**flat-leaf parsley**
1 large tomato, skinned and chopped	
½ teaspoon tabasco sauce	

Begin by draining the soaked chickpeas and place them in a saucepan with enough cold water to cover. Bring them up to simmering point, put a lid on and simmer gently for about 45 minutes or until the chickpeas are tender when tested with a skewer.

Meanwhile heat the oil in a small frying-pan and gently sauté the onion for 5 minutes, then add the garlic and cook for another 5 minutes. The spring onions should now be trimmed and chopped small and the chilli should be split, de-seeded under a cold running tap and also chopped small. Don't forget to wash your hands straight away!

When the chickpeas are ready, drain them in a sieve set over a bowl, then transfer them to a food processor along with some salt, the sautéed onion and garlic and any oil left in the pan. Now add the lime juice and blend until you have a smoothish purée – if it's too stiff add a couple of tablespoons of the cooking liquid from the chickpeas. What you need is a soft purée like hummus in texture.

Now empty the contents of the processor into a bowl and add the tomato, chilli, spring onions, tabasco, coriander and 2 tablespoons of soured cream. Taste to check the seasoning and add a few more drops of tabasco if it needs a little more kick. Cover the bowl and chill till needed. Serve garnished with black olives and some flat-leaf parsley.

———————— ◊ ————————

Cold Poached Egg Salad *with* Watercress Sauce

·

SERVES 3 AS A MAIN COURSE OR 6 AS A STARTER

*T*his is a kind of variation on the egg mayonnaise theme, but I think extremely attractive and even more delicious.

6 large fresh eggs	**2 teaspoons wine vinegar**
	1 teaspoon lemon juice
	1 teaspoon salt
FOR THE WATERCRESS SAUCE:	**freshly milled black pepper**
4 oz (110 g) watercress, dried on kitchen paper	
2 large eggs	**TO SERVE:**
1 clove garlic	**2 packets mixed green-leaf salad or any other salad leaves**
1 rounded teaspoon mustard powder	
10 fl oz (275 ml) groundnut oil	

Begin by poaching the eggs: fill a frying-pan with water to a depth of approximately 1½ inches (4 cm), then heat it to a temperature just sufficient to keep the water at a bare simmer. Then break the eggs, 2 at a time, into the simmering water and let them cook for 3 minutes or so. As soon as they're cooked to your liking, use a draining-spoon to lift them from the water and transfer them to a bowl of cold water. Then cook the remaining eggs, and leave them in the cold water while you prepare the sauce.

Separate off the watercress leaves and discard the stalks. Now break the 2 eggs into the goblet of a food processor or blender, add the salt, garlic, mustard powder and a few twists of freshly milled black pepper, then switch on to blend these together. Next pour the oil in a *thin* trickle through the hole in the top with the machine still switched on. When all the oil is in, add the vinegar, lemon juice and watercress leaves, then blend again until the sauce takes on a lovely speckled green colour.

To serve, arrange thinly sliced salad leaves round the edges of your serving-plates to form a border, then arrange 1 or 2 eggs in the centre and spoon the sauce over and around them. Serve with crusty wholemeal bread.

———— ◊ ————

CHAPTER SEVEN

SUMMER MEAT
and
POULTRY

———— ◊ ————

Summer is the best time to cook and eat home-reared lamb, because it's lamb that has had the benefit of the luscious spring grazing and tastes all the better for it. Chicken, too, is good in summer provided you look for that essential label 'free-range' – under any other circumstances the season is irrelevant and so is the flavour. It is a constant refrain of mine, but I would rather not eat meat at all if it lacks quality or taste: better to eat it less often and pay more for quality.

One of the imponderables I had to face while writing a collection of recipes for summer was the vagaries of the British climate. 'What summer?' I could hear people saying. That is the reason why the television series included a programme on 'bright meals for rainy days' and this book contains a number of more exotic recipes, like the Sri Lankan Curry which is made with coconut. If you haven't yet used fresh coconut for cooking, perhaps a rainy day is the time to get to grips with it. It's much more user-friendly than you may think (see the recipe on page 122): it really enhances curries *and* provides a delicious sambal to go with them.

————————————

Pork Saltimbocca

·

SERVES 2

This classic Italian recipe should be made with veal, but we find it tastes even nicer made with pork escalopes. Sometimes you can buy them ready prepared, but if you can't, it's very simple to prepare them yourself.

8 oz pork tenderloin, cut into 6 medallions 1 inch (2.5 cm) thick	**6 fl oz (170 ml) Marsala wine**
6 slices Parma ham – approx. 2½ oz (60 g)	**salt and freshly milled black pepper**
6 large fresh sage leaves	**You will also need a large frying-pan with base measuring 9 inches (23 cm) and 3 cocktail sticks.**
1½ tablespoons olive oil	

First of all beat the pieces of meat out to make them a little thinner. I use a clenched fist to do this, but don't go mad and break the meat – it just needs to be flattened and stretched a bit. Season the meat with salt and pepper and now lay the slices of Parma ham on top of the pork (because they won't be precisely the same size, fold them and double over the pieces if necessary to make them fit). Now place a sage leaf in the centre of each piece and secure it with half a cocktail stick, using it as you would a dress-making pin.

Next measure the Marsala into a small saucepan and place it on a gentle heat to warm through. Now heat the oil in the frying-pan until fairly hot, then fry the slices of pork (sage leaf side down first) for 2 minutes, then flip the pieces over and fry them for another 2 minutes. After that pour in the hot Marsala and let it bubble and reduce for a minute or so until it becomes a syrupy sauce. Now transfer the pork to warm serving-plates, remove the cocktail sticks and spoon the sauce over. Serve with sautéed potatoes sprinkled with a few herbs before cooking, and a mixed salad.

◊

Baked Lamb *with* Rosemary *with* Redcurrant *and* Mint Sauce

·

SERVES 6

*L*amb is in peak condition in mid-summer, as it has then had the benefit of the sweet, young, spring grazing. At this time I would only serve it plain-roasted with a sauce of young mint leaves. Later on in the summer this is a fine way to cook and serve it: the foil-baking ensures that it stays juicy.

1 × 4–4½ lb (1.8–2 kg) leg of lamb
2 tablespoons chopped fresh rosemary leaves plus 1 sprig of rosemary
1 clove garlic
10 fl oz (275 ml) dry white wine
1 tablespoon extra virgin olive oil
½ teaspoon rock salt
freshly milled black pepper

FOR THE SAUCE:
3 tablespoons good-quality redcurrant jelly
3 tablespoons red wine vinegar
4 tablespoons chopped fresh mint
salt and freshly milled black pepper

You will also need a roasting-tin.

Pre-heat the oven to gas mark 5, 375°F (190°C).

First of all crush the garlic and rock salt together to a purée, using a pestle and mortar, then add the oil, chopped rosemary and a good seasoning of pepper and mix well. Next spread a large sheet of foil over the roasting-tin, place the lamb on it and stab the fleshy parts of the joint several times with a skewer. Now spread the rosemary mixture all over the upper surface of the lamb and tuck in a sprig of rosemary (as this makes a nice garnish later).

Then bring the edges of the foil up over the lamb, make a pleat in the top and scrunch in the ends. This foil parcel should be fairly loose to allow the air to circulate. Bake the lamb for 2 hours, then open out the foil, baste the joint well with the juices and return it to the oven for a further 30 minutes to brown. The above cooking time should produce the lamb very slightly pink: you can cook it for more or less time, as you prefer.

Meanwhile make the sauce by combining the redcurrant jelly and vinegar in a small saucepan and whisking over a gentle heat till the jelly melts into the vinegar (a balloon whisk does this perfectly). Then add the chopped mint and some seasoning and pour into a jug – the sauce doesn't need to be warm.

When the lamb is cooked, remove it from the oven and allow it to rest for 20 minutes before carving. Discard the foil, spoon off the fat and make some gravy with the juices left in the tin: add the white wine, stir and let it bubble until it has become syrupy. Season with salt and pepper if it needs it and pour into a warmed serving-jug.

Baked Lamb with Rosemary with Redcurrant and Mint Sauce

Sri Lankan Curry

·

SERVES 4

This is one of my favourite curries made extra special by the use of fresh coconut, half of which goes into the curry and the rest is used to make the sambal on opposite page. If you've never used a fresh coconut before, fear not – I have given very easy, straightforward instructions on page 151.

1½ lb (700 g) shoulder or neck fillet of lamb (weighed after trimming), cut into cubes

2 onions, chopped small

1 large clove garlic, crushed

3 tablespoons groundnut oil

1½ heaped tablespoons plain flour

1 rounded tablespoon Madras curry powder

3 oz (75 g) fresh coconut, finely grated

3 oz (75 g) creamed coconut, grated

milk from 1 fresh coconut

approx. 1 pint (570 ml) stock

1-inch (2.5-cm) whole cinnamon stick

6 cardamom pods, crushed

1 rounded teaspoon fenugreek powder

salt and freshly milled black pepper

TO GARNISH:

2 hard-boiled eggs, halved

1 medium onion, quartered then separated out into layers

Pre-heat the oven to gas mark 2, 300°F (150°C).

First heat 1 tablespoon of the oil in a large casserole, then add the onions and garlic and cook gently to soften for 5 minutes. Next heat the remaining 2 tablespoons of oil in a frying-pan and, when it's nice and hot, quickly brown the cubes of meat (you will have to do this in two batches). Then sprinkle the flour and curry powder over the onions in the casserole and stir to soak up the juice, then cook gently for 2 minutes.

Now pour the coconut milk into a measuring-jug and make up to 1¼ pints (725 ml) with stock and slowly pour this into the casserole, stirring all the time. Next stir in the grated fresh and creamed coconut and transfer the browned meat to the casserole. Finally add the spices and season with salt and pepper. Bring up to simmering point, cover and cook in the centre of the oven or on a low simmer on top of the stove for 2 hours. Five minutes before the end of the cooking time, remove the cinnamon stick and stir the hard-boiled eggs and onion pieces into the curry to warm through (the onions are not meant to be cooked). Serve with the Coconut Sambal (opposite) and Spiced Pilau Rice (see page 124).

Coconut Sambal

·

SERVES 4

flesh of ½ fresh coconut, finely grated	**2 teaspoons lemon or lime juice**
1 medium onion	**½ teaspoon salt**
¼ teaspoon chilli powder	

Quite simply, grate the coconut and the onion straight into a bowl, then sprinkle in the chilli powder, the lemon or lime juice and the salt. Stir to get everything nicely blended, then sprinkle just a tiny dusting of chilli powder over the top, cover and chill slightly until needed.

———————— ◊ ————————

Spiced Pilau Rice

·

SERVES 4

The fragrance and flavour of an authentic spiced pilau rice, made with the best-quality basmati rice, is so good it could be eaten just on its own! If cooking rice bothers you, follow these instructions and you'll never have a problem.

white basmati rice measured up to the 10 fl oz (275 ml) level in a glass measuring-jug	1 small onion, finely chopped
	2 cardamom pods, crushed
	¾ teaspoon cumin seeds, crushed
boiling water measured to the 1 pint (570 ml) level in a glass measuring-jug	½ teaspoon coriander seeds, crushed
	1-inch (2.5-cm) whole cinnamon stick
	1 bayleaf
1 tablespoon groundnut oil	salt

Use a pestle and mortar to crush the cardamom pods and the cumin and coriander seeds. Then warm a 10-inch (25-cm) frying-pan (with a lid) over a medium heat, add the crushed spices (the pods as well as the seeds of the cardamom), turn the heat up high and toss them around in the heat to dry-roast them and draw out the flavour: this will take about a minute. After that add the oil and the onion and fry the onion till lightly tinged brown.

Next stir in the rice – there's no need to wash it – and turn the grains over in the pan till they are nicely coated and glistening with oil, then pour in the boiling water. Add the cinnamon, bayleaf and a good seasoning of salt, stir once only, then put the lid on, turn the heat down to its very lowest and let the rice cook for exactly 15 minutes. Don't remove the lid and *absolutely no stirring* at any stage from now on because this breaks the grains and causes them to become sticky. After 15 minutes take the pan off the heat, remove the lid and cover with a clean tea-cloth for 5 minutes before serving. Then empty the rice into a warmed serving-dish and fluff up lightly with a fork before it goes to the table.

———————— ◊ ————————

Coriander Chutney

·

SERVES 6

2 oz (50 g) fresh coriander, roughly chopped	**1 fresh chilli, de-seeded and chopped**
	1 clove garlic
1 tablespoon lime juice	**¼ teaspoon sugar**
3 tablespoons water	**salt and freshly milled black pepper**

Place half the coriander leaves in the goblet of a liquidiser, or in the small goblet of a food processor, together with the lime juice, water, chilli and garlic, then blend till smooth. You'll have to do this with a few stops to scrape down the sides of the goblet. When smooth, add the remaining coriander and continue to blend until smooth again. Taste and flavour with sugar, salt and pepper and keep in a small, covered bowl in the fridge until needed.

—————————— ◊ ——————————

Baked Thai Red Curry Chicken

·

SERVES 2

If you have some Thai Red Curry Paste (see page 59) to hand, this makes a very speedy supper dish for two (or more) people. Serve the chicken with Spiced Pilau Rice (see page 124) and Coriander Chutney (see page 125).

2 partly boned chicken breasts	**TO GARNISH:**
2 teaspoons groundnut oil	**1 lime, cut into quarters**
2 rounded tablespoons Thai Red Curry Paste (see page 59)	**a few sprigs of fresh coriander**
salt	

About 1 or 2 hours before you need to cook the chicken, lay the breasts in a heatproof dish, then take a sharp knife and make four diagonal cuts across each breast. Sprinkle first with a little salt and then with the oil, rubbing the oil well into the chicken. Next spread the curry paste over the surface of each portion and rub that in well too. Cover with clingfilm and leave on one side for the chicken to soak up all the flavours.

To cook the chicken, pre-heat the oven to gas mark 4, 350°F (180°C). Place the dish on a high shelf and cook for 30 minutes, basting with the juices from time to time. Serve the chicken with the rice and coriander chutney, as mentioned above, garnishing with sprigs of coriander and some lime quarters to squeeze over.

———————— ◊ ————————

Lamb's Liver *with* Melted Onions *and* Marsala

·

SERVES 2

Buying liver cut as thinly as one would want is always difficult, so this recipe, which calls for liver cut into thin strips, avoids the problem. If you don't have the sweet Italian Marsala wine, you could use any wine that's handy.

8 oz (225 g) lamb's liver	**2 tablespoons balsamic vinegar**
3 medium onions, halved and thinly sliced	**½ oz (10 g) butter**
	salt and freshly milled black pepper
10 fl oz (275 ml) Marsala wine	
1 large clove garlic, crushed	**You will also need**
2 tablespoons olive oil	**2 medium frying-pans.**

In the first frying-pan heat 1 tablespoon of the oil, then add the onions and, keeping the heat fairly high, toss them around to brown to a dark – almost black – colour round the edges. Then add the garlic and toss that round the pan a bit, now pour in the Marsala and balsamic vinegar. Bring everything up to simmering point, then turn the heat down to its lowest setting and let it just barely bubble (without covering) for 45 minutes. Then season with salt and freshly milled pepper.

Meanwhile prepare the liver by slicing it into approximately 1½-inch (4-cm) lengths, keeping the lengths very thin (about the size of thin French fries). When the 45 minutes are up, heat the remaining 1 tablespoon oil along with the butter in the other frying-pan and, when the butter foams, add the liver slices and sear them very briefly. They take only about 1–2 minutes to brown, so do be careful as over-cooking will dry them too much. As soon as they're ready tip them into a warmed serving-dish, pour the hot sauce and onions from the other pan over them and serve immediately. This is good served with Sliced Potatoes Baked with Tomatoes and Basil (page 73).

———————— ◊ ————————

Chicken *with* Sherry Vinegar *and* Tarragon Sauce

·

SERVES 4

This is my adaptation of a classic French dish called poulet au vinaigre. *It's very simple to make: the chicken is flavoured with tarragon leaves and simmered in a mixture of sherry vinegar and medium sherry without a lid, so that the liquid cooks down to a glossy, concentrated sauce. Serve with some well-chilled Fino sherry as an aperitif – perfect for a warm summer's evening.*

1 × 3½ lb (1.75 kg) chicken, jointed into 8 pieces, or you could use 4 bone-in chicken breast portions	2 tablespoons fresh tarragon leaves
	1 heaped tablespoon crème fraîche
5 fl oz (150 ml) good quality sherry vinegar	salt and freshly milled black pepper
15 fl oz (425 ml) medium-dry Amontillado sherry	**TO GARNISH:** 8 small sprigs of fresh tarragon
12 shallots, peeled and left whole	
4 cloves garlic, peeled and left whole	You will also need a large, roomy frying-pan 9 inches (23 cm) in diameter.
2 tablespoons olive oil	

First of all heat the oil in the frying-pan and season the chicken joints with salt and pepper. Then, when the oil begins to shimmer, fry the chicken (in two batches) to brown well: remove the first batch to a plate while you tackle the second. Each joint needs to be a lovely golden-brown colour. When the second batch is ready, remove it to the plate to join the rest. Then add the shallots to the pan, brown these a little, and finally add the garlic cloves to colour slightly.

Now turn the heat down, return the chicken pieces to the pan, scatter the tarragon leaves all over, then pour in the vinegar and sherry. Let it all simmer for a bit, then turn the heat to a very low setting so that the whole thing barely bubbles for 45 minutes. Half-way through turn the chicken pieces over to allow the other sides to sit in the sauce.

When they're ready, remove them to a warm serving-dish (right side up) along with the shallots and garlic. The sauce will by now have reduced and concentrated, so all you do is whisk the crème fraîche into it, taste and season as required, then pour the sauce all over the chicken and scatter with the sprigs of tarragon. This is lovely served with tiny new potatoes tossed in herbs and some fresh shelled peas.

——— ◊ ———

Chicken with Sherry Vinegar and Tarragon Sauce

Chicken Basque

.

SERVES 4

*T*he delicious combination of chicken and rice, olives and peppers is typical of all the regions around the western Mediterranean, but to my mind this Spanish version with the addition of spicy chorizo sausage and a hint of paprika beats the lot. My interpretation of it also uses dried tomatoes preserved in oil to give it even more character. This recipe will provide a complete supper for four from the same pot – it needs nothing to accompany it!

1 × 3½ lb (1.75 kg) chicken, jointed into 8 pieces	1 level tablespoon tomato purée
2 large red peppers	½ teaspoon hot paprika
1 very large or 2 medium onions	1 teaspoon chopped fresh herbs
2 oz (50 g) sun-dried tomatoes in oil	2 oz (50 g) pitted black olives, halved
2–3 tablespoons extra virgin olive oil	½ large orange, peeled and cut into wedges
2 large cloves garlic, chopped	salt and freshly milled black pepper
5 oz (150 g) chorizo sausage, skinned and cut into ½-inch (1-cm) slices	
brown basmati rice measured to the 8 fl oz (225 ml) level in a glass measuring-jug	You will also need a wide, shallow, flameproof casserole with a domed lid, measuring about 9½ inches (24 cm) at the base; or, failing that, any wide flameproof casserole of 8-pint (4½-litre) capacity.
10 fl oz (275 ml) chicken stock (made from the giblets)	
6 fl oz (170 ml) dry white wine	

Start off by seasoning the chicken joints well with salt and pepper. Next slice the red peppers in half and remove the seeds and pith, then slice each half into six strips. Likewise peel the onion and slice into strips of approximately the same size. The dried tomatoes should be drained, wiped dry with kitchen paper and then cut into ½-inch (1-cm) pieces.

Now heat 2 tablespoons olive oil in the casserole and, when it is fairly hot, add the chicken pieces – two or three at a time – and brown them to a nutty golden colour on both sides. As they brown remove them to a plate lined with kitchen paper using a draining-spoon. Next add a little more oil to the casserole, with the heat slightly higher than medium. As soon as the oil is hot, add the onion and peppers and allow them to brown a little at the edges, moving them around from time to time, for about 5 minutes.

After that add the garlic, chorizo and dried tomatoes and toss these around for a minute or two until the garlic is pale golden and the chorizo has taken on some colour. Next stir in the rice and, when the grains have a good coating of oil, add the stock, wine, tomato purée and paprika. As soon as everything has reached simmering point, turn the heat down to a gentle simmer. Add a little more seasoning, then place the chicken gently on top of everything (it's important to keep the rice down in the liquid). Finally sprinkle the herbs over the chicken pieces and scatter the olives and wedges of orange in among them.

Cover with a tight-fitting lid and cook over the gentlest possible heat for about 50 minutes–1 hour or until the rice is cooked but still retains a little bite. Alternatively cook in a pre-heated oven at gas mark 4, 350°F (180°C), for 1 hour.

NOTE: This recipe also works well using carnaroli rice.

———————— ◊ ————————

CHAPTER EIGHT

JELLIES, CREAMS
and
COMPOTES

◊

As a confirmed weight-watcher *and* a lover of good food I try my best to eat a dessert only when I am out for supper or at home at the weekend. But what so often disappoints me – particularly in restaurants – is that the dessert I have been anticipating with such eagerness is a real let-down. Menus nowadays contain not nearly enough fruit-based dishes, which are low on calories. Or if a dessert is going to be really rich, and squander millions of calories, it *must* be absolutely ace or it's such a waste!

For those of you with similar problems I have in this chapter set about devising recipes that are lighter and in particular make the most of all the wonderful fruits and flavours of summer. Adult jellies made with wine are great fun and look stunning (see the photograph on page 140), and oven-baked compotes seem to draw out the flavour of the fruits in a way that poaching never does. As for the creamier desserts – well, even here we've succeeded in lightening them by the use of less fatty ingredients such as fromage frais with 8 per cent fat or natural Greek yoghurt without sacrificing an iota of flavour.

Peach Wine Jellies *with* Peach Purée

·

SERVES 8

Now that there are several peach-flavoured sparkling wines on the market, they can be made into lovely jellies which retain some of the bubble and sparkle of the wine. Topped with a peach purée, they make one of the nicest, cool, light summer desserts you can imagine.

2 large or 3 small limes	a squeeze of lime juice
1 × 75 cl bottle good quality sparkling peach wine	a little caster sugar to taste
5 oz (150 g) caster sugar	**TO GARNISH:**
1 pint (570 ml) water	strawberries
3 × 0.4 oz (11 g) sachets gelatine granules	
FOR THE PEACH PURÉE:	**You will also need**
4 ripe peaches (or nectarines)	**8 × 7 fl oz (200 ml) wine glasses.**

First of all make the jelly. Take a parer or potato peeler and pare off the outer zest of the limes, being careful to take as little of the white pith as possible. Now place the lime zest in a saucepan with 1 pint (570 ml) water and the sugar and bring it up to the boil very slowly so that the lime has a chance to infuse, then remove the pan from the heat and whisk in the gelatine. Leave it to stand, whisking occasionally, until the gelatine has dissolved – about 10 minutes.

Next squeeze the juice from the limes and add it to the mixture. Pour the whole lot into a large bowl – straining out the lime zest, which is no longer needed – and leave the mixture until it becomes syrupy, which will take about 45 minutes–1 hour. After that uncork the wine and gently stir it into the jelly mixture, a little at a time. Pour the mixture into the glasses, cover each one with clingfilm and chill for several hours until set.

You need to make the peach purée just before serving. First make a cut all around each peach, then give a little twist to separate the halves. Remove the stones, then bring a saucepan of water up to the boil and pop the peach halves in for about 1 minute. After that remove them with a draining-spoon and slip the skins off. Now transfer the peaches to a food processor, add a little lime juice and caster sugar to taste (it's difficult to be specific here because peaches vary so much) and whizz them to a purée. Before serving the jellies, spoon the peach purée over the surface as a topping and garnish each one with a fresh strawberry to decorate.

Gooseberry *and* Elderflower Jellies

·

SERVES 6

Jellies have played an increasing part in my repertoire in recent years, and this is largely because you can make really excellent jellies using various fruits and wines which provide a sophisticated dessert without too many calories. This is a splendid example.

1 lb (450 g) small green gooseberries	4 tablespoons elderflower cordial
4 oz (110 g) caster sugar	(see page 150)
2 × 0.4 oz (11 g) sachets powdered gelatine	
12 fl oz (350 ml) Saumur or other sparkling wine	You will also need 6 stemmed glasses each of at least 7 fl oz (200 ml) capacity.

Begin by topping and tailing the gooseberries, then put them in a wide, shallow pan with a lid. Sprinkle the sugar over them, then place over a very gentle heat, cover and let them heat through and soften for 5–6 minutes, stirring them around a couple of times.

Meanwhile soak the gelatine in a cup with 3 tablespoons water. Then, as soon as the gooseberries are just soft, remove them from the heat and stir in the gelatine mixture – very gently so as not to break the fruit too much. Now pour the whole lot into a large bowl and leave to cool. As it cools and then becomes cold it will begin to turn syrupy (about 45 minutes–1 hour), and at this stage pour in the elderflower cordial and the wine. Mix thoroughly and then pour the jelly into the stemmed glasses. Cover them with clingfilm and chill in the refrigerator till you need them (I use a small baking-tin as a tray to put the glasses on and this makes it much easier to keep them together in the refrigerator). Serve the jellies as they are or else with a blob of fromage frais on the top decorated with a small sprig of mint.

———————— ◊ ————————

Italian Rice Creams
with Gooseberry *and* Elderflower Purée

·

SERVES 6

For those who get nostalgic for the rice puddings of their childhood, this is the adult answer, a more sophisticated and modern interpretation. Later on in the summer different fruits can be used for the purée – blackcurrants, raspberries and redcurrants, or any other combination.

3 oz (75 g) Italian arborio rice
3 oz (75 g) caster sugar
1½ pints (850 ml) full-cream milk
½ oz (10 g) butter
5 fl oz (150 ml) whipping cream
4-inch (10-cm) strip lemon zest
3 drops of pure vanilla extract
¼ whole nutmeg, freshly grated
1 × large egg yolk
2 level teaspoons powdered gelatine

FOR THE GOOSEBERRY AND ELDERFLOWER PURÉE:

12 oz (350 g) gooseberries
2 oz (50 g) caster sugar
2 tablespoons elderflower cordial

TO GARNISH:

sprigs of mint

You will also need 6 × 5 fl oz (150 ml) ramekins, 3 inches (7.5 cm) across and 1½ inches (4 cm) deep, lightly buttered.

First pour the milk into a saucepan and add the sugar, nutmeg and lemon zest. Stir and bring everything up to simmering point, then add the rice, giving it several good stirs. Then turn the heat down to its very lowest setting, put a lid on and leave it for about 40–50 minutes, giving it a stir every now and again. If your heat is not low enough you may need to use a heat diffuser (see page 195). What you need to end up with is a mixture where most of the liquid has been absorbed.

About 10 minutes before the end of the cooking time measure the cream into a jug and whisk the gelatine into it to soak. Then, when the rice is ready, pour the cream and gelatine mixture into it, followed by the egg yolk, butter and vanilla extract, and stir to mix everything very thoroughly, still keeping the heat very low. When it is all heated through – after about 2 minutes – remove from the heat and pour the mixture into the ramekins. Leave them to cool completely, then cover with clingfilm and chill till needed.

To make the gooseberry and elderflower purée, simply place the goose-berries and sugar in a saucepan over a very gentle heat. Cover with a lid and allow the gooseberries to come up to simmering point to release their juices. Cook for 5–6 minutes or until the skins are soft. Then put the whole lot into a blender and whizz to a purée, or else press through a nylon sieve. When cool, stir in the cordial, then cover and chill till needed.

To turn out the rice creams, slide a small palette knife round the edges and ease away from the sides using your finger. Invert on to small serving-plates by giving a hefty shake. Serve with gooseberry and elderflower purée poured over, and garnish with sprigs of mint.

———————— ◊ ————————

A Terrine *of* Summer Fruits

·

SERVES 8

*T*his one is a stunner – see for yourself in the photograph. It's also dead easy to make and slices like a dream – a lovely, fresh-tasting summer dessert. Note: it's important to have two tins because the terrine needs to be weighted whilst it is setting.

15 fl oz (425 ml) sparkling rosé wine
2 × 0.4 oz (11 g) sachets gelatine granules
2 oz (50 g) caster sugar
1 tablespoon fresh lime juice

FOR THE FRUIT:

12 oz (350 g) small strawberries
8 oz (225 g) raspberries

4 oz (110 g) each of blackcurrants, redcurrants and blueberries (or any other combination you like)

You will also need 2 × 2 lb (900 g) loaf tins, 7½ × 4¾ inches × 3½ inches deep (19 × 12 cm × 9 cm deep), preferably non-stick but anyway with a good surface.

First prepare the fruit: remove the stalks; and halve the strawberries if they are any larger than a quail's egg. Then mix the fruits together in a large bowl, being very gentle so as to avoid bruising them.

Now in a small saucepan heat half the rosé wine till it begins to simmer, then whisk the sugar and gelatine into it. Make sure that everything has dissolved completely before adding the remaining wine and the lime juice. Then pour the liquid into a jug and allow it to cool. While that's happening, lay the mixed fruit in the loaf tin – and it's worth arranging the bottom layer with the smallest prettiest-shaped fruit as this will be on top when the terrine is turned out.

Next pour all but 5 fl oz (150 ml) of the liquid over the fruit. Now lay a sheet of clingfilm over the tin, place the other tin directly on top, then put two unopened tins of tomatoes or something similar to act as weights into the top tin and put the whole lot into the fridge for about 1 hour or until it has set. Then warm up the remaining 5 fl oz (150 ml) wine mixture and pour it over the surface of the terrine. Re-cover with clingfilm and return to the fridge overnight to set firm.

When you are ready to serve, turn out the terrine by dipping the tin very briefly in hot water and inverting it on to a plate. Use a very sharp knife (also dipped first into hot water) to cut it into slices. Serve with chilled pouring cream, crème fraîche or Greek yoghurt.

NOTE: In testing I have found that it is necessary to add the smaller amount of jelly at the end to avoid spillage when weighting as it's this weighting which makes the terrine easy to slice.

A Terrine of Summer Fruits

Summer Fruit Compote

·

SERVES 6

*A*ny mixture of fruit can be used for this, but remember that the flavour of blackcurrants does tend to dominate – so, if you're using them, just use a half-quantity compared with the other fruits.

3 peaches
6 apricots
6 large plums
8 oz (225 g) blueberries
6 oz (175 g) raspberries
2 oz (50 g) sugar

You will also need a shallow baking-dish: I used a round dish approx. 12 inches (30 cm) in diameter.

Pre-heat the oven to gas mark 4, 350°F (180°C).

First prepare the fruit. Halve each peach by making a slit all round through the natural crease, then simply twist in half and remove the stone. Cut the halves into three pieces each and place them in the baking-dish. After that do the same with the apricots and, if they're large, slice the halves into two; if they're small, leave the halves whole. Repeat this with the plums, but if they're clinging too tightly to their stones you may find it easier to slice them into quarters on the stone and pull each quarter off.

Add the apricots and plums to the peaches in the dish, followed by the blueberries. Now sprinkle the sugar over them, place the dish in the centre of the oven and let the fruits bake (without covering) for 25–30 minutes or until they are tender when tested with a skewer and the juices have run. Then remove them from the oven and gently stir in the raspberries, tipping the bowl and basting them with the hot juices. Taste to check the sugar and add more if you think it needs it, then cool the compote and chill in the fridge. Serve with crème fraîche, or this is wonderful with the Quick Nougatine Ice Cream (page 163).

NOTE: If you want to make the compote entirely with soft berries, it needs only 10 minutes in the oven.

Summer Fruit Compote Scented *with* Lemon Grass

·

SERVES 6

This is unusual and subtle – the scent of the lemon grass is barely there, but it does add a very interesting dimension.

Any fruit compote combination (see page 142)	2 finger-thin stems lemon grass, trimmed (see page 18)
	2 oz (50 g) caster sugar

Cut the lemon grass into 1-inch (2.5-cm) pieces and place them in the small goblet of a food processor or a liquidiser together with the sugar. Turn the motor on and process until the lemon grass is so small that it disappears into the sugar. Add this mixture to the fruit and cook as described on page 142, remembering to add soft fruit only after cooking.

◊

Vanilla Cream Terrine *with* Raspberries *and* Blackcurrant Coulis

·

SERVES 6

T*his is one of those oh-so-simple-but-oh-so-good desserts that offers precisely the right background to vivid, rich fruit like blackcurrants.*

FOR THE TERRINE:	TO GARNISH:
15 fl oz (425 ml) whipping cream	6 oz (175 g) raspberries
3 oz (75 g) caster sugar	fresh mint leaves
1½ × 0.4 oz (11 g) sachets gelatine powder	
15 fl oz (425 ml) Greek yoghurt	You will also need a plastic box measuring 4 × 4 × 4 inches (10 × 10 × 10 cm).
2 teaspoons pure vanilla extract	

FOR THE BLACKCURRANT COULIS:

8 oz (225 g) blackcurrants
3 oz (75 g) caster sugar

Begin by placing the gelatine in a cup together with 3 tablespoons of the cream and leave it to soak for 10 minutes. Meanwhile place the rest of the cream in a saucepan with the sugar and heat gently till the sugar has dissolved (it's important not to over-heat the cream). Next add the soaked gelatine to the warm cream and whisk everything over the heat for a few seconds. Now remove the cream mixture from the heat.

In a mixing-bowl stir the yoghurt and vanilla together, then pour in the gelatine cream mixture through a sieve. Mix very thoroughly and pour the whole lot into the plastic box, allow to cool, then cover and chill in the fridge for at least 4–6 hours or preferably overnight until it's set.

Meanwhile make the blackcurrant coulis by first de-stalking the blackcurrants and then sprinkling them with the sugar in a bowl. Leave to soak for 30 minutes, and then you can either sieve them directly back into the bowl or, to make the sieving easier, process them first then sieve into the bowl. Taste to check that you have added enough sugar, then pour into a jug and chill until you're ready to serve the terrine.

To serve, turn the terrine out on to a board, first sliding a palette knife around the edges to loosen it, then give it a hefty shake to turn it out and cut into six slices. Arrange each slice on a serving-plate, spoon a little blackcurrant coulis over the top right-hand corner and the bottom left-hand corner of each one and decorate with the fresh raspberries and mint leaves.

Vanilla Cream Terrine with Raspberries and Blackcurrant Coulis

Rhubarb Compote

·

SERVES 3

Sometimes the simplest recipe can be a star if it's done properly. Rhubarb suffers from being over-boiled and smashed to a pulp, but if you cook it gently in the oven with just sugar and no water, it will slowly release its juice, keep its chunky shape – and taste wonderful.

Use 1½ lb (700 g) rhubarb with 3 oz (75 g) caster sugar, and bake in a shallow baking-dish, without covering, in a pre-heated oven at gas mark 4, 350°F (180°C), for 30–40 minutes. For other variations you could add the grated zest and juice of 1 large orange, or 1 heaped teaspoon of grated fresh ginger (the ginger flavour works best, I think, with soft brown rather than white sugar).

VARIATIONS
Rhubarb Yoghurt Fool

For this simple but so-lovely dessert, make a Rhubarb Compote as above, then whizz it to a purée in a food processor together with 1 × 7 fl oz (200 ml) tub real Greek yoghurt. Garnish with some preserved ginger or a slice of orange.

Gooseberry Yoghurt Fool

This is made with exactly the same quantities, and using the same method, as Rhubarb Compote then puréed with the yoghurt as above.

Compote *of* Fresh Figs *in* Muscat Wine *with* Vanilla Custard

·

SERVES 4

Imported figs are rarely ripe and ready-to-eat, so a good way to serve them is lightly poached in a sweet, raisiny Muscat wine – Beaumes de Venise, or else a more modest Spanish or Italian equivalent.

8 plump fresh figs	**FOR THE CUSTARD:**
½ bottle (37.5 cl) Muscat wine	**1 vanilla pod (after using for the figs)**
1 strip of lemon zest	**10 fl oz (275 ml) milk**
1 vanilla pod	**3 × large egg yolks**
	1 rounded teaspoon cornflour
	1 tablespoon mild honey

What you need to do is select a saucepan or frying-pan, with a lid, large enough to hold the figs in a single layer. Pour the wine into the pan and add the lemon zest and vanilla pod and bring it up to simmering point. Now wash the figs and stab each one two or three times with a skewer, then, using a long-handled spoon, lower them into the simmering liquid, stalk side up. Cover and cook very gently for 5–10 minutes or until they are absolutely tender.

Now use a draining-spoon to remove them from the liquid to a shallow serving-dish where again they can sit in a single layer. Then scoop out the lemon zest and the vanilla pod (reserving this for use later) and boil the liquid rapidly until it has reduced to half its original volume. Pour it over the figs, leave to cool and chill until needed.

To make the custard, wipe the vanilla pod, split it down its length and place it in a saucepan along with the milk. Heat it very gently and, while it's heating, whisk the egg yolks, cornflour and honey together in a basin. When the milk has come slowly up to boiling point, remove the vanilla pod and pour the hot milk on to the egg mixture, whisking it in as you pour. Then return the whole mixture to the saucepan and put it back on the heat, whisking gently until it has thickened and almost reached boiling point. Now pour the custard into a jug, cover with clingfilm, leave to cool and then chill. Remove from the fridge 1 hour before serving. Serve handed round to pour on to the figs.

NOTE: Vanilla pods can be wiped clean, stored in a jar and used again and again.

Fresh Peaches Baked *in* Marsala *with* Mascarpone Cream

·

SERVES 6

This combination of fresh, ripe peaches and the luscious flavour of Marsala wine makes a supremely good summer dessert that has the added advantage of being made well in advance. Mascarpone cream cheese has a rich dairy flavour, but it does tend to be a bit heavy, so mixing it with an equal quantity of fromage frais lightens the texture without losing the flavour.

FOR THE PEACHES:
1½ oz (40 g) caster sugar
6 firm ripe peaches
10 fl oz (275 ml) sweet Marsala wine
1-inch (2.5-cm) cinnamon stick
1 vanilla pod
1 rounded teaspoon arrowroot

FOR THE MASCARPONE CREAM:
4 rounded tablespoons mascarpone (Italian cream cheese)

4 rounded tablespoons 8 per cent fromage frais
a few drops of pure vanilla extract
1 dessertspoon caster sugar

You will also need a shallow baking-dish.

Pre-heat the oven to gas mark 4, 350°F (180°C).

Begin by halving the peaches and removing their stones, then place the halves in a bowl, pour boiling water over them and, after 30 seconds, drain them and slip off their skins. Now place the peach halves in the shallow baking-dish, rounded side down, mix the sugar and Marsala in a jug and pour it over the peaches. Add the cinnamon stick and vanilla pod to the dish, then place it on the centre shelf of the oven and bake without covering for 35–40 minutes. Then remove the peaches from the oven and drain off all the juices into a small saucepan. Mix the arrowroot with a little cold water and then add it to the saucepan and whisk over a gentle heat until slightly thickened. This will happen as soon as it reaches simmering point. Then pour it back over the peaches and leave to cool. Cover and refrigerate for 24 hours to allow the flavour to develop fully.

To make the mascarpone cream, simply beat all the ingredients together thoroughly and pile into a pretty serving-bowl to hand round separately.

———— ◊ ————

Fresh Peaches Baked in Marsala

Ingredients Update

One of the great benefits of cooking today is that between the large chain supermarkets and the specialised foodshops we can all literally shop around the world. Sometimes, however, the pace at which new and unusual ingredients are presented to us can be quite daunting. So on these pages I am offering a few notes by way of introduction to the less familiar ingredients which you'll find in some of the recipes.

I realise that mentioning a product on television or in a book can create a problem because things then sell out very quickly. But it is only when we build up a demand that suppliers will respond – then absolutely everyone can get whatever it is instead of just the privileged few.

FRESH LEMON GRASS

The British have always taken quickly to the flavours of the orient. Thai cooking, in particular, has grown enormously in popularity of late and thus introduced us to the fragrant stalks of lemon grass. It's not exactly a lemon flavour, but the strong scent is noticeably citrus.

When you buy it lemon grass looks most uninviting but the flavour is sublime. We add it to a very English summer fruit compote and it gives it a marvellously different dimension.

FRESH CORIANDER

Fresh coriander is another new and different flavour. It has a peculiar effect on people: they often begin by not liking it much at all and end up being totally addicted to it – so please don't give up too early.

Although the flavour of fresh coriander is quite reminiscent of tne crushed coriander seeds which we're more familiar with, it is much stronger and more pungent, so a little goes a long way.

ROCKET LEAVES

Unlike the two items above, rocket has been firmly rooted in traditional British cooking since Elizabethan times. Although most designer salad leaves are visually pleasing, they so often lack guts and flavour. Rocket is quite the opposite – it has a really full-bodied buttery and leafy flavour. Mixed with other leaves, or simply on its own, it is currently my number one favourite salad leaf. What we need, please, is for more English growers to take it seriously and provide us with a constant supply.

ELDERFLOWER CORDIAL

Elderflowers have a wonderful affinity with gooseberries – and nature has kindly matched their seasons for us – but until recently only those who are lucky enough to live in the country and can gather them away from the petrol-fumed roadside have been able to enjoy this delightful combination. Not so now, because there is available to all (from supermarkets and wine shops) an excellent cordial distilled from elderflowers, which makes combining them with gooseberries as easy as pouring them from a bottle. You may also be interested to know that it makes a superb non-alcoholic drink: one measure of cordial topped with sparkling mineral water and lots of ice. Most refreshing.

CRÈME FRAÎCHE

Thankfully crème fraîche is now a standard item in large supermarkets. Not so heavy as double cream, it has a lower fat content and so fewer calories. It may be lighter but it is still thick and luxurious, wonderful with summer fruits and excellent for cooking since it doesn't curdle easily.

MASCARPONE

This luscious Italian cream cheese is 90 per cent fat, and wickedly wonderful. In Italy they sometimes thin it down with the addition of beaten eggs, but we have discovered a way to retain the richness and flavour yet at the same time lighten the texture and reduce the fat content. How? Simply combine it with an equal quantity of 8 per cent fromage frais. Again it makes a lovely topping for fruit compotes and is equally good for sandwiching meringues together.

PURE VANILLA EXTRACT
So much vanilla is sold nowadays in the form of an essence, which is often a synthetic creation. Always look for the pure extract: the best is available from specialised food shops or by post from Lakeland Plastics (address on page 195). The quality does make an enormous difference in recipes where a vanilla pod is unsuitable.

FRESH COCONUT
Dealing with a fresh coconut (which does not, I admit, look user-friendly) is not as difficult as it seems.

First push a skewer into the three holes in the top of the coconut and drain out the milk and reserve it if the recipe needs it. Then place the coconut in a polythene bag and sit it on a hard surface – a stone floor or an outside paving stone. Then give it a hefty whack with a hammer – it won't be that difficult to break. Now remove the pieces from the bag and using a cloth to protect your hands, prise the tip of a kitchen knife between the nut and the shell. You should find you can force the whole piece out in one go. Now discard the shell and take off the inner skin using a potato peeler. The coconut is now ready to use.

COCONUT PRODUCTS
In the television series we extolled the virtues of fresh coconuts at some length. What is really good news for cooks is that we can now buy creamed coconut packed in bars, which can be grated into curries or melted in milk. Similarly powdered coconut is more widely available. It doesn't sound very glamorous, but it's a gem in making ice creams, puddings and cakes and even for cooking with rice. Both are musts for a serious cook's store-cupboard.

TURRON
Turron is a delicious confection, rather like crisp nougat. It's made with toasted almonds and comes in bars from larger supermarkets. If I'm in an indulgent or celebratory mood I can easily sit and eat a whole bar straight off, but it is also great in the kitchen crushed and then sprinkled over ice cream or actually used to make ice cream (see page 163). It was introduced into Europe by the Moors and is made primarily in Italy (where it is called 'torrone') and Spain – we think the Spanish variety has the edge.

COUS-COUS
Anyone who likes pasta will like cous-cous, which *is* pasta but made into tiny particles. It doesn't need any cooking; just soaking in hot water or brief steaming. There's something about the lightness of cous-cous that makes it a very summery ingredient. We have used it both as a basis for a beautiful salad (see page 108) and as a crust for oven-baked salmon (page 52).

CHEESES
There are three examples of the more unusual cheeses in this book. The first is Greek *halloumi*, not the most exciting cheese to nibble but one that cooks very well and absorbs other flavours. We have served it fried with a delicious sauce (page 16), and also transformed it into kebabs (see page 90) to put on to the barbecue (for the poor vegetarians who so often miss out on such occasions).

The second cheese is *Pecorino Romano*. This is an Italian sheep's cheese, similar in look and texture to Parmesan but not so expensive. Its sharpness and coarseness make it extremely good in all sorts of pasta dishes.

Finally there is *smoked mozzarella*, a creamy fast-melting cheese with a lovely smokiness to it that gives it a more distinctive flavour than the plain variety.

BLACK ONION SEEDS
Dark and exotic, these can be sprinkled over salads or used as a topping for breads and rolls. They are available from most supermarkets and from Asian food shops.

CHAPTER NINE

I CES
and
GRANITAS

———— ◊ ————

This is a huge subject and this chapter can do no more than offer you an introduction and encouragement to go more deeply into it. At long last there is a splendidly comprehensive book, *Ices* by Robin Weir and Caroline Liddell (published by Hodder & Stoughton), which is crammed with wonderful recipes and tells you absolutely everything you need to know about the subject. It is one area of eating that has grown meteorically in recent years, and after generations of uninspired factory-made ice creams we are now seeing some very sophisticated and well-made versions popping up everywhere from ice-cream stalls to supermarkets.

Yet, however good they are, nothing can beat a home-made ice cream, and you can now buy an ice-cream maker for about £50, which cuts down the time you need to spend attending to the freezing process. Nevertheless, even without a machine, hiking the ice out of the freezer and giving it a quick whisk isn't really a bother provided you set a timer to remind you to do it! The only other thing you must remember to do is to transfer the ice cream to the fridge to allow it to soften before serving. These times will vary, but are given in each recipe. I shouldn't really be partial because all the recipes in this chapter are favourites of mine, but if you want to give yourself a treat try the Gooseberry and Elderflower Ice Cream (page 160) and serve it with the English Gooseberry Cobbler (page 187): a winning combination!

NOTES ON MAKING ICE CREAM
Ice-cream Makers

There are several ice-cream makers now available. The most efficient – and expensive – kind makes the ice cream from start to finish in approximately 30–40 minutes. This has its own built-in freezing device, therefore all you then do is transfer the finished ice cream to a polythene box for storing in the fridge till needed. If you're an ice-cream addict and make a lot of home-made ice cream, it would be worth the expense, though remember that machines always need somewhere to live, and space could be a problem.

The second kind of ice-cream maker is simply a machine that does the churning. The canister that holds the ice cream while it's churning has to be stored in the freezer and removed only when you need to actually churn it. The mixture then goes in and the machine churns it for 30–40 minutes, until the ice cream is thick. Then it is transferred to a polythene box for freezer storage if it's not going to be eaten straight away. The canister is then washed, dried and returned to the freezer until next needed for ice-cream making. It requires at least 12 hours in the freezer to become capable of freezing, and often – if a large quantity of ice cream is needed in one go – it's worth having two canisters so that you always have a standby. They come in 2- or 2½-pint (1.1- or 1.5-litre) sizes (or with slight variations according to the make). What is important is that the size of the canister must be larger than the amount of ice cream, because during churning the volume increases.

Making Ice Cream without an Ice-cream Maker (Freezer Method)

To make ice cream without an ice-cream maker you need a shallow polythene box (with a lid) of 3½ pints (2 litres) capacity – this works out at 8 × 8 inches × 2½ inches deep (20 × 20 cm × 6 cm deep). The shallowness enables the freezing to happen more quickly and also makes whisking easier as the beater can go down straight into the box.

It's a very easy process: all you do is pour the mixture into the box, put the lid on and place it in the freezer for about 3–4 hours (it's impossible to be too precise because freezers vary). What you need is a mixture that is half-frozen – the particles round the edges will be frozen solid but the centre will still be soft. At this stage you remove it from the freezer and using a hand-whisk beat the frozen bits back into the soft bits till you get a uniform texture. Then the lid goes back on and the ice cream is frozen again and the same process repeated 3 hours later. After the second beating the ice cream is ready and can be returned to the freezer until it's needed. Incidentally it's a good idea to arm yourself with a digital kitchen timer to remind you to remove the ice cream and whip it at various stages.

Serving Ice Cream

Serving ice cream is another of those minefields where guidelines are tricky because fridge temperatures vary. All I can do is remind you that the standard fridge temperature is 41°F (5°C) – you can buy fridge thermometers to check this. Assuming that your fridge *is* 41°F then, unless otherwise stated in the recipe, the average time for an ice cream to 'come back' from being frozen is 40 minutes in the refrigerator. Don't be tempted to speed this up by by-passing the fridge and putting it straight into room temperature as all this does is melt the outside edges and leave the centre rock-hard.

——————— ◊ ———————

Strawberry Granita

·

SERVES 8

*T*his is the recipe to make when there's a real glut of ripe strawberries. It's a much nicer way to conserve them than simply freezing them. It looks like sparkling jewels when you serve it in tall glasses – and it contains hardly any calories!

1 lb (450 g) ripe strawberries
6 oz (175 g) caster sugar
1 pint (570 ml) water
3 tablespoons lemon juice

You will also need a polythene freezer box 8 × 8 inches × 2½ inches deep (20 × 20 cm × 6 cm deep).

First hull the strawberries, then put them in a colander and rinse them briefly with cold water. Drain well and dry them on kitchen paper before transferring them to a food processor or liquidiser. Blend them to a smooth purée, then stop the motor, add the sugar and blend again very briefly. After that add the water and lemon juice, blend once more, then pour everything into a fine nylon sieve set over a bowl. Rub the purée through the sieve, then pour it into the polythene freezer box, cover with a lid and put into the freezer for 2 hours.

By that time the mixture should have started to freeze around the sides and base of the container, so take a large fork and mix the frozen mixture into the unfrozen, then re-cover and return to the freezer for another hour. After that repeat with another vigorous mixing with a fork, cover again and re-freeze for a further hour. At this stage the mixture should be a completely frozen snow of ice crystals, and is ready to serve. It can remain at this servable stage in the freezer for a further 3–4 hours, but after that the ice will become too solid and it will need putting in the main body of the fridge for 30–40 minutes or until it is soft enough to break up with a fork again.

I like to serve the granita in small, narrow, unstemmed glasses – but any wine glasses will do so that the sparkling colour can be seen in all its glory.

———————— ◊ ————————

Strawberry Granita

Caledonian Ice Cream

·

SERVES 8

This is, quite simply, a knock-out ice cream – one of the best I've ever tasted. I am indebted to the Ubiquitous Chip restaurant in Glasgow, which very kindly let me have the recipe. The nutty, caramelised oatmeal gives a wonderful flavour and texture to the ice cream and the whole thing makes a sublime partner to all summer fruits and compotes.

FOR THE CARAMELISED OATMEAL:	FOR THE ICE CREAM:
3 oz (75 g) caster sugar	1 pint (570 ml) whipping cream
4 tablespoons water	½ teaspoon pure vanilla extract
2 oz (50 g) pinhead oatmeal	

FOR THE SYRUP:	You will also need a loaf tin measuring 7½ × 4½ inches × 3½ inches deep (19 × 11 cm × 9 cm deep) and a small baking-sheet brushed with oil.
4 oz (110 g) caster sugar	
4 tablespoons water	

Start off by making the caramelised oatmeal. Put the 3 oz (75 g) caster sugar and 4 tablespoons of water in a small saucepan over a low heat and leave it for 5 minutes. Then take a medium-sized frying-pan, place it on a medium heat and, when the pan is hot, add the oatmeal and swirl it round the pan constantly so that it browns evenly – which it will do in about 5 minutes. Remove the oatmeal to a plate to prevent it becoming over-brown. By now the sugar in the saucepan will have dissolved, so you can turn the heat right up and let it boil (watching it like a hawk) until it begins to turn a rich caramel colour, rather like dark runny honey.

As soon as it reaches that stage, stir in the toasted oatmeal, remove from the heat and quickly pour the mixture over the oiled baking-sheet, then leave it on one side to get cold and firm (approx. 15 minutes). Now take off small pieces at a time and pound them with a pestle and mortar until the mixture resembles something the size of salt crystals. Place them in a bowl and keep covered until you're ready to make the ice cream.

To make the sugar syrup, measure the sugar and water into a small saucepan, place it over a gentle heat and stir until the sugar has dissolved – about 5 minutes. Then remove it from the heat and allow it to get completely cold.

Now to make the ice cream. Pour the cold syrup into a mixing-bowl along with the whipping cream, add the vanilla and whisk with an electric hand-whisk until the mixture just begins to thicken and hold its shape. Then pour this mixture into an ice-cream maker and freeze-churn until it is firm but still pliable – this will take about 30–40 minutes. Now transfer it to a bowl and fold in the oatmeal mixture evenly, then spoon it into the tin, cover with a double thickness of foil and freeze till needed.

To serve, remove from the freezer to the refrigerator about 20 minutes before you need it. Then dip the base and sides of the tin in hot water for 20 seconds or so, loosen all round the edges with a palette knife, then turn out on to a plate. Using a sharp knife dipped into hot water, cut the ice cream into slices and serve on large plates with either soft fruit or any of the compotes or coulis on pages 142–6.

If you don't have an ice-cream maker you can make this ice cream as described on page 155 – except that in this particular case the caramelised oatmeal must be folded in just before the final freezing.

VARIATION

Macadamia Praline Ice Cream

This can be made as above but with 6 oz (175 g) of crushed Macadamia Nut Brittle (page 171) in place of the oatmeal mixture.

———— ◊ ————

Gooseberry *and* Elderflower Ice Cream

·

SERVES 6–8 MAKES 2 PINTS (1.2 LITRES)

This ice cream is unbelievably good. Perhaps one of the best treats of early summer would be to serve the English Gooseberry Cobbler (page 187) accompanied by this gooseberry ice cream: what a combination!

1½ lb (700 g) young green gooseberries	2 oz (50 g) sugar
3 oz (75 g) sugar	1 dessertspoon liquid glucose
8 tablespoons elderflower cordial	1 rounded teaspoon cornflour

FOR THE CUSTARD:	**You will also need a 3½-pint (2-litre) polythene freezer box 8 × 8 inches × 2½ inches deep (20 × 20 cm × 6 cm deep).**
10 fl oz (275 ml) whipping cream	
3 × medium egg yolks	

First place the cream in a saucepan and bring it up to just below simmering point. While it is heating, place the egg yolks, 2 oz (50 g) sugar and the cornflour in a bowl and whisk together till smooth. Now add the liquid glucose to the hot cream and whisk that too until the glucose has melted down and blended with the cream. Next, pour the whole lot over the egg mixture, then return everything to the saucepan and continue whisking over a medium heat until the mixture thickens to a custard. Now rinse out and dry the bowl, pour the custard back in, cover with clingfilm and allow to cool.

Meanwhile top and tail the gooseberries using kitchen scissors and place them in a saucepan with 3 oz (75 g) sugar. Put a lid on the pan, place over a low heat and let them cook gently till soft – about 5–6 minutes. Then place a large nylon sieve over a bowl and press the gooseberries through to extract all the pips.

Next, stir the elderflower cordial into the gooseberry purée and, as soon as the custard is cool enough, combine the two together. Now you can either freeze-churn the mixture in an ice-cream maker till thick, or else pour it into the polythene freezer box, cover with a lid and freeze till half-frozen (about 3–4 hours). At this stage beat the mixture, still in the box, with an electric hand-whisk. Return it to the freezer, then repeat 3 hours later, and after that freeze till solid and store till needed. Transfer to the main body of the fridge for 30 minutes before serving.

◊

Lemon Meringue Ice Cream

.

SERVES 8–10 MAKES 2½ PINTS (1.5 LITRES)

This is sharp, very lemony and most refreshing, truly an ice cream for summer. We have found that the shop-bought meringues actually work better than home-made ones for this as they retain their crunchiness – which does make the whole thing easier to make!

4 meringue nests, broken into coarse chunks

FOR THE LEMON SYRUP:
7 fl oz (200 ml) fresh lemon juice (4–5 lemons)

grated zest of 2 lemons

5 oz (150 g) caster sugar

2 heaped teaspoons cornflour

FOR THE ICE CREAM:
4 × medium egg yolks

6 oz (175 g) caster sugar

15 fl oz (425 ml) whipping cream

7 fl oz (200 ml) Greek yoghurt

1 rounded teaspoon cornflour

You will also need a 3½-pint (2-litre) polythene freezer box
8 × 8 inches × 2½ inches deep (20 × 20 cm × 6 cm deep).

First of all make the lemon syrup: in a bowl mix the cornflour with 2 tablespoons of the lemon juice. Then in a small saucepan dissolve the sugar with the remaining lemon juice over a low heat (5–6 minutes), add the zest, bring up to simmering point and cook for 5 minutes. Pour this over the cornflour mixture, return it all to the pan and, still keeping the heat low, cook for 2 more minutes, stirring, until thickened. Then cool and leave on one side till required.

Now make the custard base for the ice cream. Place the cream in a saucepan and heat gently. Meanwhile whisk the egg yolks, cornflour and sugar together, then, when the cream reaches simmering point, pour it over the other ingredients, still whisking, and return the whole lot to the saucepan and bring back to a bare simmer, continuing to whisk. Pour the thickened custard into a bowl, cover with clingfilm placed directly on the surface of the custard and leave on one side until cold.

When the mixture is cold, combine it with the yoghurt, then pour this into the freezer box, cover and freeze for 2 hours or until the mixture is starting to freeze. After that use an electric hand-whisk to whisk again, while it is still in the box. Re-freeze, then after a couple of hours repeat the whisking, this time adding the lemon syrup. Finally lightly and evenly fold in the meringue pieces, put the lid back on and freeze till needed. It will take a further 6–8 hours to freeze completely.

NOTE: The quantity of this ice cream is too much for a standard ice-cream maker.

Rhubarb Crumble Ice Cream

·

SERVES 6–8 MAKES 2 PINTS (1.2 LITRES)

*I*t has to be said that while we were filming ice creams for the television series, the team tasted them all (with not a spoonful left over!) and voted this one their number one favourite.

FOR THE ICE CREAM:

1 lb (450 g) trimmed rhubarb
15 fl oz (425 ml) whipping cream
8 oz (225 g) sugar
1 tablespoon lemon juice

FOR THE CRUMBLE:

3 oz (75 g) plain white flour
2 oz (50 g) butter
2 oz (50 g) light brown muscovado sugar
½ level teaspoon ground ginger

You will also need a shallow, 11 × 7-inch (28 × 18-cm) baking-tin and a 3½-pint (2-litre) polythene freezer box 8 × 8 inches × 2½ inches deep (20 × 20 cm × 6 cm deep).

Pre-heat the oven to gas mark 5, 375°F (190°C).

First of all make the crumble by combining all the ingredients together in a bowl and using your hands to rub the butter into the flour so that the mixture comes together to form small, pea-sized balls of dough (rather as if someone had made a half-hearted attempt to make breadcrumbs from very fresh bread!). Now sprinkle this evenly into the baking-tin and leave on one side.

Now cut the rhubarb into ½-inch (1-cm) lengths and place them in a large, shallow baking-dish along with the sugar and lemon juice. Place the dish on a lower shelf in the pre-heated oven and the tin containing the crumble mixture on the shelf above. The crumble needs to be baked for 10 minutes, then remove it from the oven and leave to cool. The rhubarb may need a further 15–20 minutes' cooking before it is completely tender: when it's cooked, take it out and leave it to cool a little before pouring it into a food processor or blender. Process until you have a smooth purée, then pour it into a measuring-jug, cover and transfer to the fridge to chill.

Before making the ice cream, use your hands to break up the cooled crumble and restore it to small, pea-sized pieces (if they're too big, the pieces are unwieldy to eat in the ice cream; if they're too small, they disappear). Next stir the cream into the rhubarb purée, pour into an ice-cream maker and churn until the mixture has the consistency of softly whipped cream. Quickly spoon it into the polythene freezer box and stir in the crumble pieces. Put the lid on, then freeze for a minimum of 2 hours or until the ice cream is firm enough to serve.

To make without an ice-cream maker, freeze the mixture (without the crumble) in the box for 3–4 hours, then whisk and return to the freezer. Re-freeze for a further 2 hours, then whisk again and stir in the crumble before the final freezing. (See page 154 for notes on ice cream.)

If frozen solid, the ice cream will need to be transferred to the main body of the fridge for about 25 minutes before serving to allow it to become soft enough to scoop.

———————— ◊ ————————

Quick Nougatine Ice Cream

·

SERVES 6–8 MAKES 1¾ PINTS (1 LITRE)

If you hunt through the sweet section at a large supermarket, you will find a very hard, crisp almond confection called Torrone from Italy or Turron from Spain. There is a softer, chewy version, but for ice cream the crisp crunchy version is best. Crushed into ice cream, the result is superb.

4 × large egg yolks	**1 rounded teaspoon cornflour**
3 oz (75 g) sugar	
15 fl oz (425 ml) milk	
10 fl oz (275 ml) fromage frais	**You will also need a 3½-pint**
2 teaspoons pure vanilla extract	**(2-litre) polythene freezer box**
2 × 100 g bars Turron	**8 × 8 inches × 2½ inches deep**
	(20 × 20 cm × 6 cm deep).

First whisk the cornflour, egg yolks and sugar together in a bowl until thick. Then heat the milk in a saucepan till it is just boiling and pour it over the egg mixture, whisking the whole time. Now transfer it all back to the saucepan and heat, keeping the heat low and stirring all the time, until the mixture thickens, but don't let it quite come up to the boil. After that add the vanilla, then pour it all into a bowl and allow it to cool completely.

Meanwhile break up the Turron into pieces approximately ¼ inch (5 mm) square. When the custard mixture is quite cold, fold the fromage frais and the Turron into it. Transfer to an ice-cream maker and churn for 20–30 minutes or according to the machine instructions. Spoon the ice cream into the polythene freezer box and freeze till needed, transferring it to the fridge 30 minutes before serving. To make this without an ice-cream maker, see the instructions on page 155. This is excellent served with any berry fruits or one of the compotes on pages 142–3 and 146.

———————— ◊ ————————

Ice-cream Sodas

An ice-cream soda is a cross between a drink and a sundae. For children this can simply be a matter of placing two scoops of ice cream into a sundae glass (or a tumbler will do), pouring over 3 fl oz (75 ml) of cordial and adding a bottle of soda water – which will give it a beautiful frothy head.

Instead of soda and cordial you could pour in Coca-cola or authentic lemonade for the same effect: what it must have is some fizz. You'll need to give everyone a straw and a long spoon.

For a more special ice-cream soda, make up some lemon syrup as for Home-made Lemonade (see page 95) and assemble as above.

◊

Hot Fudge Sundae

.

SERVES 6

This is the most sublime summer chocolate dessert, especially for eating out of doors – say, at a barbecue.

18 scoops of Very Easy Vanilla Ice Cream (see page 170)

FOR THE FUDGE SAUCE:
1 × 170 g tin evaporated milk
8 oz (225 g) good-quality plain chocolate

FOR THE TOPPING:
3 oz (75 g) mixed nuts (pecans, brazils, almonds, peanuts, hazelnuts, on their own or in combination), coarsely chopped and lightly toasted
6 dessertspoons whipping cream or crème fraîche

The sauce can be made at any stage and kept covered in the fridge, then re-heated. All you do is pour the evaporated milk into a small basin, then break up the chocolate into small squares and add them to the milk. Place the basin on a saucepan of barely simmering water and leave it to melt, stirring from time to time. It will take about 10 minutes to become a lovely fudgy mass.

To serve the sundaes, put three scoops of very firm, cold ice cream per person into tall glasses, followed by 3 dessertspoons of hot fudge sauce, followed by 1 dessertspoon whipped cream or crème fraîche. Finally sprinkle over some chopped nuts and serve absolutely immediately.

◊

Ice-cream Soda

Strawberry Cheesecake Ice Cream

·

SERVES 8–10 MAKES 2½ PINTS (1.5 LITRES)

This is what I'd call half-dessert and half-ice cream. My niece Hannah and nephew Tom are chief ice-cream tasters in our family and this one gets very high ratings indeed. It differs from others in this chapter in that it needs 2 hours in the main body of the fridge – at 41°F (5°C) – to become soft enough to scoop, so don't forget to allow time for that. It won't taste nearly as good if it hasn't been allowed to soften.

FOR THE ICE CREAM:
4 × medium egg yolks
3 oz (75 g) caster sugar
1 lb (450 g) medium-fat curd cheese
5 fl oz (150 ml) whipping cream
5 fl oz (150 ml) Greek yoghurt
1 rounded teaspoon cornflour
1 teaspoon pure vanilla extract
1 tablespoon fresh lemon juice

FOR THE STRAWBERRY PURÉE:

8 oz (225 g) fresh strawberries, hulled

2 oz (50 g) caster sugar
2 fl oz (55 ml) hot water

FOR THE CRUMBLE MIXTURE:

2 oz (50 g) sweet oat biscuits
1 oz (25 g) butter, melted
½ oz (10 g) chopped toasted hazelnuts

You will also need a shallow baking-tray and a 3½-pint (2-litre) polythene freezer box 8 × 8 inches × 2½ inches deep (20 × 20 cm × 6 cm deep).

First of all prepare the strawberry purée. Make a sugar syrup by placing 2 oz (50 g) caster sugar and 2 fl oz (55 ml) water in a small saucepan. Put it on a gentle heat and allow the sugar to dissolve completely, stirring from time to time – this will take about 5–6 minutes. When there are no sugar granules left, let it come to simmering point and simmer very gently for 5 minutes. Now pile all the strawberries into a food processor, add the syrup and blend to a smooth purée. Then strain the purée through a nylon sieve into a bowl to extract the seeds.

Now, to make the crunchy bits for the ice cream, pre-heat the oven to gas mark 5, 375°F (190°C). Crush the biscuits with a rolling-pin – not too finely – then place them in a bowl and combine them with the hazelnuts and 1 oz (25 g) melted butter. Mix everything together, spread the mixture out on the shallow baking-tray and bake on the top shelf of the oven for exactly 5 minutes: put the timer on and watch carefully, because any more than 5 minutes will be too long. Then remove it from the oven and allow to cool.

Next you need to make the custard base for the ice cream, and to do this place the cream in a saucepan and heat gently. Meanwhile whisk the egg yolks, cornflour and sugar together, then when the cream reaches simmering point, pour it over the egg yolk mixture (still whisking). Return the whole lot to the saucepan and bring back to a bare simmer, keeping up the whisking until the custard thickens slightly. Pour it into a bowl, cover with clingfilm placed right on the surface of the custard and leave on one side till cold.

After that place the curd cheese, yoghurt, vanilla and lemon juice in a mixing-bowl, add the cooled custard and whisk the whole lot together till smooth. Now either freeze churn the mixture in an ice-cream maker until thickened, then, transfer to the polythene freezer box and quickly fold in the crumble mixture followed by the strawberry purée, which should form ribbons of red through the ice cream. Freeze for 5–6 hours. Or if you do not have an ice-cream maker, pile the custard and cheese mixture into the polythene freezer box and freeze for approximately 3 hours (see page 155). Then whisk again till soft. Re-freeze and repeat the process after 2–3 hours, then fold in the crumble mixture followed by the strawberry purée as described above. Return the ice cream to the freezer box and freeze till needed. Transfer to the main body of the fridge 2 hours before serving.

———————— ◊ ————————

Coconut Ice Cream

·

SERVES 4–6 MAKES 1½ PINTS (850 ML)

A lthough coconut milk powder doesn't sound very nice it is actually a brilliant product and makes excellent ice cream. Serve it with Lime Syrup (page 170) – the combination is superlative.

3 × large egg yolks	**½ teaspoon pure vanilla extract**
4 oz (110 g) caster sugar	**1 rounded teaspoon cornflour**
5 level tablespoons coconut milk powder	
15 fl oz (425 ml) milk	**You will also need a polythene freezer box 6 × 8 inches × 2 inches deep**
2½ fl oz (65 ml) whipping cream	**(15 × 20 cm × 5 cm deep).**

First, in a mixing-bowl, whisk the egg yolks, cornflour and sugar together until thick and creamy. Then, in a saucepan, warm the milk and, as it warms, gradually add the coconut milk powder, whisking to dissolve it into the milk. Now pour the hot milk mixture over the egg yolks, return the whole lot to the saucepan and cook for 1 minute, stirring, until the mixture thickens. It is important to keep stirring to make sure that the mixture does not 'catch' on the bottom of the pan. Then return it all to the bowl and allow it to become completely cold.

To make the ice cream, whisk the cream until it thickens slightly, then stir it, together with the vanilla extract, into the custard mixture. Transfer it all to the polythene freezer box and put in the coldest part of the freezer for 2 hours or until it becomes firm at the edges. At this stage empty it out into a mixing-bowl and whisk again with an electric hand-whisk to break down the ice crystals. Return to the freezer, repeat the whisking process after another 2 hours, then re-freeze until needed. Place in the fridge for 1 hour before serving. This can, of course, be made in an ice-cream maker following the manufacturer's instructions.

◊

Coconut Ice Cream with Lime Syrup (page 170)

Lime Syrup

·

MAKES 10 FL OZ (275 ML)

*T*his is extremely simple to make and keeps well so it can be made in advance. Serve it with Coconut Ice Cream (page 168) or the Ice-cream Sodas (page 164).

4 oz (110 g) sugar	**4 fl oz (110 ml) fresh lime juice**
4 fl oz (110 ml) water	**(approx. 3 limes)**
zest of 1 lime (removed with a potato peeler), cut into very fine strips	**1 level teaspoon arrowroot**

Begin by putting the sugar and water into a small, heavy-based saucepan, bring it very slowly up to a simmer, then stir to dissolve the sugar. Add the zest of lime and simmer very gently for 15 minutes without reducing the volume. Meanwhile mix the arrowroot with the lime juice in a cup and, when the syrup is ready, pour it in, stirring all the time. Continue to heat it over a gentle heat, and allow it to come back to simmering point – by then it will have thickened very slightly and become clear. Leave the syrup to cool and store it in the fridge in a sealed container: it keeps well for several days.

Very Easy Vanilla Ice Cream

·

SERVES 8–10 MAKES 2½ PINTS (1.5 LITRES)

2 × 10 fl oz (275 ml) tins condensed milk	**You will also need a 3½-pint**
10 fl oz (275 ml) single cream	**(2-litre) polythene freezer box**
2 × 7 oz (200 ml) cartons crème fraîche	**8 × 8 inches × 2½ inches deep**
2 teaspoons pure vanilla extract	**(20 × 20 cm × 6 cm deep).**

Simply put everything into a bowl and use an electric hand-whisk to mix all the ingredients thoroughly. Then pour the mixture into the polythene freezer box and place it in the coldest part of the freezer. After about 2 hours, or when the edges are starting to freeze, remove it and use the hand-whisk to give it another good mix and break down any ice crystals. Return to the freezer, then repeat the whisking after 3 more hours. Finally return it to the freezer for a further 6–8 hours, by which time it should be at serving consistency. If you've made it a long time ahead and it's very hard, transfer it to the main body of the fridge for 30 minutes to soften enough to scoop.
NOTE: Because of the sugar content in condensed milk this recipe is not suitable for ice-cream makers.

Macadamia Nut Brittle

Although you can buy nut brittle nowadays, it's extra specially good if you make it yourself. It keeps well wrapped in foil in the fridge, so you can take out a little at a time to crush and sprinkle over ice creams. Any nuts can be used, but my personal favourite at the moment are macadamia nuts which somehow seem more summery!

4 oz (110 g) macadamia nuts
8 fl oz (225 ml) water
1 lb (450 g) granulated sugar

You will also need a solid baking-sheet and a 9-inch (23-cm) plate, lightly oiled.

Pre-heat the oven to gas mark 4, 350°F (180°C).

Begin by spreading the nuts out over the baking-sheet. Place it in the oven for 8–10 minutes or until the nuts are just pale golden (do put a timer on, and watch carefully, as too much browning will spoil the flavour).

Next have ready a bowl filled with cold water, and a tea-towel to hand, then proceed as follows: put the sugar in a heavy-based saucepan over a very gentle heat and measure in 8 fl oz (225 ml) of water. Then stir constantly to dissolve the sugar in the water. If a lot of sugar crystals stick to the side of the pan, use a wet pastry brush to brush them back down. You need to be very patient here and keep the heat low until all the sugar has completely dissolved – and this can take 10–15 minutes.

After that you can stop stirring, bring the sugar up to the boil, and boil until it is a light caramel colour (the colour of runny honey). If you are using a sugar thermometer this will be when it reaches 340°F (170°C) and will take 10–12 minutes, but don't go away as it needs constant watching.

When it is ready, cover your hand with a cloth in case of splashes and put the base of the pan into the water in the bowl to stop the sugar cooking. Now add the nuts and, as soon as the mixture has stopped bubbling, pour it on to the lightly oiled plate. If it goes brittle before it is out of the pan, put it back on the most gentle heat, then quickly pour it on to the plate. When it has cooled a little you can press the nuts fully into the caramel, and when it is quite cold remove it from the plate and store in the fridge wrapped in foil.

NOTE: If your saucepan looks as though it is caramelised for good, fear not: fill it with warm water and place over a gentle heat till the caramel melts away from the base and sides.

CHAPTER TEN

SUMMER BAKING
and
DESSERTS

◊

The recipes in this chapter are basically aimed at complementing the glorious fruits of summer. And what better to do that than some good, old-fashioned farmhouse fruit pies now and then? Lately I've discovered a much easier way to make a fruit pie and that is what American cookbooks call the 'one-crust' pie. No special tins or plates are needed; all you do is pile your fruit on to a large, thin sheet of shortcrust pastry and simply fold it round the fruit, leaving some of the fruit exposed in the centre (see the photograph on page 184). A good idea for a dull or rainy day is to use it to stock up on weighed-out quantities of shortcrust for the freezer so that you can make a fruit pie at a moment's notice all through the summer.

Then, when the soft fruits – the strawberries and raspberries, the redcurrants and blackcurrants – come into season, I can think of nothing nicer to serve with them than meringues. This time I've rung the changes and devised a Caramel Meringue (page 178), which is sandwiched together not with double cream but with a delectable mixture of Italian mascarpone and fromage frais, which retains the *flavour* of the mascarpone but cuts down the high fat content.

Summer tea out in the garden is one of our most civilised pastimes, and there are several ideas here for making that a bit special: muffins, for instance, the mini versions which also make use of summer fruits like blueberries or apricots. Or try the superb Coconut Lime Cake (page 188), which underlines what a perfect combination of flavours coconut makes with lime.

Preceding page: Summer Fruit Millefeuille (see opposite)

Summer Fruit Millefeuille

.

SERVES 6

You can use shop-bought puff pastry for this – it won't have such a good flavour as the quick flaky pastry below which is made with butter, but the caramelising will help the flavour and it does cut down on the time.

FOR THE CARAMELISED FLAKY PASTRY:

4 oz (110 g) flour with a pinch of salt added

2½ oz (60 g) butter, weighed carefully (too much makes too soft a pastry), wrapped in foil and left in the freezer for 1 hour

1 tablespoon lemon juice

1 egg, beaten

2 level tablespoons icing sugar

FOR THE PASTRY CREAM FILLING:

1 × large egg plus 1 egg yolk

1 oz (25 g) caster sugar

¾ oz (20 g) plain flour

7 fl oz (200 ml) whole milk

¾ teaspoon pure vanilla extract

FOR THE FRUIT:

5 oz (150 g) raspberries, hulled

5 oz (150 g) strawberries, hulled

2 oz (50 g) redcurrants, stalks removed

TO FINISH:

5 fl oz (150 ml) double cream

1 rounded tablespoon caster sugar

icing sugar for dusting

You will also need a baking-sheet, greased.

To make the pastry, first sift the flour and salt into a bowl, then take the butter from the freezer and, holding it with foil, dip it into the flour and grate it on the coarsest blade of a grater – dipping it into the flour once or twice more until it is all in the bowl. Now take a palette knife and flick the flour over the grated butter, cutting and tossing until the flour and butter look evenly blended. Next sprinkle in the lemon juice, then, using your hands, gently bring the dough together, adding a few drops of water to make a firm dough that leaves the bowl clean. Wrap it in a polythene bag and chill it in the fridge for 30 minutes. Meanwhile pre-heat the oven to gas mark 7, 425°F (220°C).

Next take a rolling-pin and a tape measure, and roll the pastry out to a square measuring 12 × 12 inches (30 × 30 cm). Using the rolling-pin to roll the pastry round, carefully transfer it to the baking-sheet. Prick the surface of the pastry with a fork and brush it all over with beaten egg, then place the baking-sheet on a high shelf in the oven and bake for 10–12 minutes – but do watch it carefully (no answering the phone, etc.), because ovens do vary. What you need is a very brown, crisp finish.

Then, to get it extra-crisp, pre-heat the grill to its highest setting, sprinkle it with 1 level tablespoon of the icing sugar and then literally flash it under the hot grill – don't take your eyes off it till the sugar caramelises, which it will do in just a few seconds.

Remove the pastry square from the grill and, using a sharp knife, cut it into three equal strips. Turn them over, sprinkle the rest of the icing sugar over and flash them under the grill once again. Once the pastry has cooled on a wire rack it is ready to use and can be stored in a polythene box with each layer separated with a strip of greaseproof paper. The pastry is very delicate, so handle it carefully, but if any strips do happen to break, don't panic – you can use them as bottom or middle layers of the millefeuille.

To make the pastry cream, break the egg into a medium-sized mixing-bowl, then add the egg yolk and sugar. Next put the milk on to warm over a gentle heat while you whisk the eggs and sugar together until the mixture becomes thickened and creamy – about 1 minute with an electric hand-whisk on first speed. Then sift in the flour and whisk that in.

Now turn the heat up to bring the milk to boiling point and then whisk the milk into the mixture. After that return the whole lot to the pan and continue to whisk, this time with a balloon whisk, over a medium heat until the mixture becomes very thick – keep the whisk going all the time because the mixture can catch very easily if you don't. As soon as a bubble on the surface bursts, remove the sauce from the heat and quickly pour it into a bowl, then stir in the vanilla extract. Cover the pastry cream with clingfilm to prevent a skin forming and leave it to get completely cold.

When you come to assemble the millefeuille (which shouldn't be before about an hour before you want to serve it), whip the double cream and caster sugar together till fairly stiff, then fold the pastry cream into it. To assemble, place the bottom layer of pastry on a suitably-sized plate or board and spread it with a quarter of the cream. Top this with half the fruit and a further quarter of the cream. Now place the next layer of pastry on top, pressing it gently down to fix it in place, and cover this with another layer of cream followed by the rest of the fruit and the rest of the cream. Finally arrange the last layer of pastry on top, dust with icing sugar and serve cut into thin slices using your sharpest knife.

———————— ◊ ————————

Fromage Frais Cheesecake *with* Strawberry Sauce

.

SERVES 8

Whenever I see cheesecake on a menu I'm filled with longing – there's something awfully comforting about cheesecake – but the question always arises as to whether it will or will not be cloying (and if it is, what a waste of calories!). This version is definitely not cloying: it's light in texture and, made with fromage frais, a bit lighter on the calories too.

FOR THE BASE:

6 oz (175 g) sweet oat biscuits (any of several types available)

2 oz (50 g) butter, melted

2 oz (50 g) coarsely chopped toasted hazelnuts

FOR THE FILLING:

12 oz (350 g) full-fat curd cheese

12 oz (350 g) fromage frais (8 per cent)

3 × medium eggs

6 oz (175 g) caster sugar

1 teaspoon pure vanilla extract

FOR THE TOPPING:

1½ lb (700 g) strawberries, hulled

2 level tablespoons caster sugar

You will also need a 9-inch (23-cm) springform baking-tin.

Pre-heat the oven to gas mark 2, 300°F (150°C).

Begin by crushing the biscuits in a food processor or with a rolling-pin, then mix them with the melted butter and stir in the hazelnuts. Now press the mixture into the base of the tin and pop it into the fridge to firm up while the filling is made.

For this combine, in a large bowl, the curd cheese, fromage frais, eggs, sugar and vanilla using an electric hand-whisk to beat everything together until silky smooth. Now pour this mixture over the biscuit base and place on the centre shelf of the oven to cook for 30 minutes. At the end of the cooking time turn out the oven but leave the cheesecake in the cooling oven to set until it's completely cold (I find that this is the best method as it prevents cracking). Remove the cheesecake from the oven and from the tin, transfer it to a plate, cover and chill till needed.

For the topping, weigh out 8 oz (225 g) of the strawberries into a bowl, sprinkle them with the caster sugar and leave to soak for 30 minutes. After that pile the strawberries and the sugar into a food processor and purée, then pass the purée through a nylon sieve to remove the seeds. To serve the cheesecake, arrange the remaining strawberries all over the surface, then spoon some of the purée over them and hand the rest of the purée separately.

Caramel Meringues

·

MAKES 12 SINGLE MERINGUES

I'm quite sure that nothing, but nothing, provides a better accompaniment to the tart flavours of soft summer fruits than meringues, light as a whisper on the outside and with a marshmallow chewiness inside. This year we've been making caramel meringues, which are even nicer and never fail to produce gasps of delight when they appear.

FOR THE CARAMEL:
2 oz (50 g) granulated sugar

FOR THE MERINGUES:
3 × large fresh egg whites
4 oz (110 g) caster sugar

TO SERVE:
**8 fl oz (225 ml) whipped cream
or crème fraîche or clotted cream
or Mascarpone Cream
(see page 148)**

You will also need a baking-sheet measuring 15 × 15 inches (38 × 38 cm), lined with non-stick silicone baking parchment.

Pre-heat the oven to gas mark 2, 300°F (150°C).

First make the caramel. Put the granulated sugar in a small, heavy saucepan and place it on a gentle heat – and stay watching it like a hawk: the sugar will eventually melt and dissolve. You can shake the pan, but don't stir. When the sugar becomes liquid let it cook until it turns the colour of dark runny honey, then take the pan off the heat immediately. Now pour the caramel on to a plate and as soon as it becomes cool enough to handle – set but not hard – loosen it from the plate, so that when it's completely hard it doesn't stick. After that break it into pieces and grind it to a fine powder with a pestle and mortar.

To make the meringues, place the egg whites in a clean bowl and, using an electric hand-whisk, whisk them until they form soft peaks that just slightly tip over when you lift the whisk. Next whisk in the caster sugar, a tablespoon at a time, followed by the caramelised sugar, also a tablespoon at a time.

When everything is thoroughly blended, take dessertspoons of the mixture and arrange these on the baking-sheet, then place a second dessert-spoon of meringue on top of each one, to make twelve meringues in all. Then place them in the oven and straight away reduce the heat to gas mark 1, 275°F (140°C), and leave them for 1 hour 15 minutes. After that turn out the oven and allow the meringues to cool inside until the oven is completely cold.

To serve, sandwich the meringues together with whipped cream, crème fraîche, clotted cream or Mascarpone Cream and serve them piled high – preferably on a cake stand – with fruit compote in a separate bowl.

American Muffins

·

MAKES 20 MINI OR 6 MAN-SIZED MUFFINS

I love American home cooking, and one of the things I feel Americans are particularly good at is baking (both at home and commercially). The American muffin reigns supreme – not like the British bread version but more like superior fairy cakes and oh so much easier to make and more of a treat. Like many other things in America they used to come big, but now that calorie-counting is here to stay there are mini versions, which means you can make lots of different bite-sized flavours. Although I think minis are more fun, it has to be admitted that my husband's cricket team prefer something more substantial, so I've given you a choice. The single basic mix will provide twenty mini or six man-sized muffins.

FOR THE BASIC MUFFIN MIXTURE:
5 oz (150 g) plain flour
½ level tablespoon baking powder
¼ teaspoon salt
1 × medium egg
1½ oz (40 g) caster sugar
4 fl oz (110 ml) milk
2 oz (50 g) butter, melted and cooled slightly
½ teaspoon pure vanilla extract

You will also need 2 mini muffin trays, each cup measuring about 1¾ × ¼ inches (45 × 5 mm), or standard English muffin tins. The muffins can be baked with or without cake papers, which simply help to keep them fresh. For stockists see page 194.

Pre-heat the oven to gas mark 6, 400°F (200°C).

Start off by sifting the flour, baking powder and salt into a large bowl. Then in a separate bowl mix together the egg, sugar, milk, melted butter and vanilla extract. Now return the dry ingredients to the sieve and sift them straight on to the egg mixture (this double sifting is essential because there won't be much mixing going on). What you need to do now is take a large spoon and fold the dry ingredients into the wet ones – quickly, in about 15 seconds. Don't be tempted to beat or stir, and don't be alarmed by the rather unattractive, uneven appearance of the mixture: this, in fact, is what will ensure that the muffins stay light.

Now fold whichever combination of fruits/nuts etc. you have chosen (see pages 181–2) into the mixture, again with a minimum of stirring: just a quick folding-in. Spoon in just enough mixture to fill each muffin cup (if you're not using papers, grease the tins well) and bake on a high shelf of the oven for 20 minutes for minis or 30 minutes for the larger ones or until well risen and brown.

Remove the muffins from the oven and cool in the tins for 5 minutes before transferring to a wire rack (if they are in paper cases remove them from the tins straight away). Leave to get quite cold before icing.

———————— ◊ ————————

Blueberry *and* Pecan Muffins

·

MAKES 20 MINI OR 6 MAN-SIZED MUFFINS

1 quantity Basic Muffin Mixture (see page 179)	**FOR THE TOPPING:**
	2 oz (50 g) pecan nuts, finely chopped
4 oz (110 g) small blueberries	**10 demerara sugar cubes, crushed**
2 oz (50 g) pecan nuts, finely chopped	

Fold the blueberries and pecan nuts into the muffin mix as described on page 179, spoon into the cases and top with chopped pecans and crushed sugar before putting into the oven.

◊

Fresh Apricot *and* Pecan Muffins *with* Cinnamon Icing

·

MAKES 20 MINI OR 6 MAN-SIZED MUFFINS

1 quantity Basic Muffin Mixture (see page 179), using half wholewheat and half plain flour	**½ teaspoon pure vanilla extract**
4 oz (110 g) fresh apricots, finely chopped	**FOR THE CINNAMON ICING:**
	3 oz (75 g) icing sugar, sifted
1 oz (25 g) pecan nuts, finely chopped and lightly toasted	**2 teaspoons ground cinnamon**
	3 teaspoons water
½ level teaspoon ground cinnamon	**10 toasted pecan nuts, cut in half**

Fold the apricots, pecan nuts and cinnamon into the muffin mixture, as indicated in the recipe on page 179. For the icing, mix the icing sugar with the water and cinnamon and spoon a little on to each muffin when they are cold, then top with half a pecan nut.

◊

Blueberry and Pecan Muffins

Coffee *and* Walnut Muffins

·

MAKES 20 MINI OR 6 MAN-SIZED MUFFINS

1 quantity Basic Muffin Mixture (see page 179)	**FOR THE TOPPING:**
3 oz (75 g) walnuts, finely chopped	**4 oz (110 g) icing sugar, sifted**
2 level tablespoons instant coffee mixed with 1 tablespoon boiling water	**2 teaspoons instant coffee mixed with 1 tablespoon boiling water**
	10 walnut halves, chopped in half again

Fold the chopped walnuts and coffee mixture into the muffin mix as described on page 179, spoon into the cases and place in the oven. For the topping, blend the coffee mixture with the icing sugar, then spoon a little on to each muffin when they are quite cold. Top with a piece of walnut.

———————————— ◊ ————————————

Blueberry *and* Cinnamon Muffin Cake *with* Struesel Topping

·

SERVES 8–10

H*aving recently got totally hooked on making muffins, I realised that the muffin mixture could be baked in an ordinary cake tin and served cut into thick slices – either as a dessert fresh and still warm from the oven and topped with Greek yoghurt, or as a cake for tea in the garden on a sunny day.*

10 oz (275 g) plain flour	**1 oz (25 g) butter, at room temperature**
1 level tablespoon baking powder	
½ teaspoon salt	**1 level teaspoon ground cinnamon**
10 oz (275 g) blueberries	**1 × 2 oz (50 g) packet chopped toasted hazelnuts**
3 oz (75 g) caster sugar	
½ teaspoon ground cinnamon	**1 tablespoon cold water**
6 fl oz (170 ml) milk	
2 × medium eggs	
4 oz (110 g) butter, melted	

You will also need a 9-inch (23-cm) springform baking-tin, lined with silicone baking parchment.

FOR THE TOPPING:

3 oz (75 g) demerara sugar

3 oz (75 g) self-raising flour

Pre-heat the oven to gas mark 5, 375°F (190°C).

As with the basic muffins you need to sift the dry ingredients twice, so place the flour, baking powder, salt and cinnamon in a sieve and sift them into a bowl. In another mixing-bowl whisk the eggs, sugar and milk together, then melt the butter and pour this into the egg mixture, whisking once again.

Now sift the flour mixture in on top of the egg mixture and fold it in, using as few folds as possible (ignore the lumpy appearance at this stage and don't be tempted to over-mix). Fold in the blueberries and spoon into the tin.

To make the topping you can use the same bowl that the flour was in. Add the flour, cinnamon and butter and rub the butter in until crumbly, then add the sugar and hazelnuts and mix well. Finally sprinkle in 1 tablespoon of cold water, then press the mixture loosely together. Now sprinkle this mixture all over the cake. Bake on the centre shelf of the oven for 1 hour 15 minutes or until it feels springy in the centre. Allow it to cool in the tin for 30 minutes before removing the sides of the tin. Then slide a palette knife gently under the base and transfer the cake to a wire rack to finish cooling.

NOTE: I have several times placed the base of a springform tin the wrong way up by mistake, so be careful that you have it the right way up!

———— ◊ ————

A Very Easy
One-crust Pie

·

SERVES 6

T*his American idea for making a pie is blissfully easy − no baking tins, and no lids to be cut, fitted and fluted. It looks very attractive because you can see the fruit inside, and because there is less pastry it's a little easier on the waistline.*

FOR THE SHORTCRUST PASTRY:
6 oz (175 g) plain flour
1½ oz (40 g) lard, at room temperature
1½ oz (40 g) butter or margarine, at room temperature
cold water

FOR THE FILLING:
1½ lb (700 g) prepared fruit (rhubarb, gooseberries, cherries, peaches, apricots, raspberries, plums or damsons − in fact anything at all!)

3 oz (75 g) caster sugar
2 rounded tablespoons semolina
1 small egg yolk

FOR THE GLAZE:
1 small egg white
6 sugar cubes, crushed

You will also need a solid baking-sheet, lightly greased.

Make up the pastry by sifting the flour into a large mixing-bowl, then rubbing the fats into it lightly with your fingertips, lifting everything up and letting it fall back into the bowl to give it a good airing. When the mixture reaches the crumb stage, sprinkle in enough cold water to bring it together to a smooth dough that leaves the bowl absolutely clean, with no crumbs left. Give it a little light knead to bring it fully together, then place the pastry in a polythene bag in the fridge for 30 minutes.

After that pre-heat the oven to gas mark 6, 400°F (200°C). Then roll the pastry out on a flat surface to a round of approximately 14 inches (35 cm): as you roll, give it quarter-turns so that it ends up as round as you can make it (don't worry, though, about ragged edges: they're fine). Now carefully roll the pastry round the rolling-pin and transfer it to the centre of the lightly greased baking-sheet.

To prevent the pastry getting soggy from any excess juice, paint the base with egg yolk (you'll need to cover approximately a 10 inch (25 cm) circle in the centre), then sprinkle the semolina lightly over this. The semolina is there to absorb the juices and the egg provides a waterproof coating.

Now simply pile the prepared fruit in the centre of the pastry, sprinkling it with sugar as you go. Then all you do is turn in the edges of the pastry: if any breaks, just patch it back on again − it's all meant to be ragged and

A Very Easy One-crust Gooseberry Pie

interesting. Brush the pastry surface all round with the egg white, then crush the sugar cubes with a rolling pin and sprinkle over the pastry (the idea of using crushed cubes is to get a less uniform look than with granulated). Now pop the pie on to the highest shelf of the oven and bake for approximately 35 minutes or until the crust is golden-brown. Remove from the oven and serve warm with chilled crème fraîche or ice cream.

NOTES ON ONE-CRUST FRUIT PIES
Other Rhubarb Variations
Try one of the following variations on the plain fruit filling: add the grated zest of 2 oranges or 1 rounded teaspoon grated fresh ginger (or powdered ginger) and soft brown sugar.

Gooseberries
Use 3 oz (75 g) sugar to sweeten and serve with Gooseberry and Elderflower Ice Cream (page 160).

Cherries
Use a hazelnut pastry made with 6 oz (175 g) plain flour, 2 oz (50 g) ground hazelnuts, ¼ teaspoon powdered cinnamon and fats as above. Use only 1½ oz (40 g) sugar to sweeten the fruit.

Apricots
Use pastry as above, with 1½ lb (700 g) apricots, stoned and quartered, plus 1 oz (25 g) toasted slivered almonds.

Raspberries and Redcurrants
Use pastry as above, with 1¼ lb (675 g) raspberries, 4 oz (110 g) redcurrants and 2 oz (50 g) sugar to sweeten.

Plums
Use pastry as above, with 1½ lb (700 g) plums, stoned and quartered, and 2 oz (75 g) sugar to sweeten.

Blackcurrants
Use 1½ lb (700 g) blackcurrants and 2 oz (75 g) sugar to sweeten.

Blackberry and Apple
Use 1 lb (450 g) apples, 8 oz (225 g) blackberries and 2 oz (75 g) sugar to sweeten.

———— ◊ ————

English Gooseberry Cobbler

·

SERVES 6

This is a classic English version of a fruit cobbler, but speeded up with the aid of a food processor – which makes it one of the fastest baked fruit desserts imaginable.

2 lb (900 g) young green gooseberries, topped and tailed	**6 fl oz (170 ml) buttermilk or fresh milk**
4 oz (110 g) caster sugar	**6 demerara sugar cubes, crushed coarsely, or 1 heaped teaspoon loose sugar**
2 tablespoons elderflower cordial (see page 150)	

FOR THE TOPPING:	
8 oz (225 g) plain flour, sifted	**You will also need a baking-dish approx. 9 inches in diameter and 2½ inches deep (23 cm and 6 cm deep).**
½ teaspoon salt	
3 level teaspoons baking powder	
4 oz (110 g) ice-cold butter or margarine, cut into pieces	Pre-heat the oven to gas mark 7, 425°F (220°C).

All you do is arrange the fruit, sugar and elderflower cordial in the baking-dish, then get on with the topping. Place the sifted flour, salt, baking powder and butter (first cut into chunks) into the goblet of a food processor. Then switch on and give it a pulse (on/off) action several times until the mixture resembles fine breadcrumbs. Then pour in the buttermilk and switch on again briefly until you have a thick, very sticky dough.

Now spoon tablespoons of the mixture over the fruit – the more haphazardly you do this, the better. Lastly sprinkle the crushed sugar over the top of the dough, then pop the dish on to a high shelf in the oven for 25–30 minutes or until it is a crusty golden-brown. Serve it warm from the oven with (if you really want a treat) Gooseberry and Elderflower Ice Cream (page 160).

VARIATIONS
Rhubarb
Use 2 lb (900 g) rhubarb and add the grated zest of an orange to the fruit, and the grated zest of ½ orange to the dough. Use the same quantity of sugar to sweeten the fruit.

Mixed Fruit
Use 2 lb (900 g) mixed fruit – peaches, apricots, plums, raspberries – with 2 oz (50 g) sugar.

Coconut Lime Cake

.

SERVES 8

6 oz (175 g) self-raising flour	**FOR THE ICING:**
6 oz (175 g) caster sugar	**8 oz (225 g) icing sugar**
6 oz (175 g) soft margarine or butter	**3 limes**
3 × large eggs, lightly beaten	
2 oz (50 g) desiccated coconut	**You will also need 2 × 8-inch (20-cm) sponge tins 1½ inches (4 cm) deep, the bases lined with silicone baking parchment.**
2 level tablespoons dried coconut milk powder	
zest and juice of 2 limes	
1 rounded teaspoon baking powder	Pre-heat the oven to gas mark 3, 325°F (170°C).

For the cake, start off by grating the zest of the 2 limes on to a small saucer, then cover that with clingfilm and set on one side. Next measure the desiccated coconut into a small bowl, then squeeze the juice of the limes and pour this over the coconut to allow it to soften and soak up the juice for an hour or so.

To make the cake, just take a large, roomy bowl and sift in the flour, lifting the sieve up high to give the flour a good airing. Then simply throw in all the other ingredients, including the lime zest and soaked coconut, and, with an electric hand-whisk switched to high speed, whisk everything till thoroughly blended – about 2–3 minutes.

Now divide the mixture equally between the two prepared tins, smooth to level off the tops and bake on a middle shelf of the oven for 30–35 minutes or until the centres feel springy to the touch. Allow the cakes to cool in the tins for 5 minutes, then turn them out on to a wire rack to cool, carefully peeling off the base papers. They must be completely cold before the icing goes on.

To make the icing, begin by removing the zest from the limes – this is best done with a zester as you need long, thin, curly strips that look pretty. Then, with your sharpest knife, remove all the outer pith then carefully remove each segment (holding the limes over a bowl to catch any juice), sliding the knife in between the membrane so that you have the flesh of the segments only. This is much easier to do with limes than it is with other citrus fruits. Drop the segments into the bowl and squeeze the last drops of juice from the pith.

Now sift the icing sugar in on top of the limes a little at a time, carefully folding it in with a tablespoon in order not to break up the lime segments too much. When all the sugar is incorporated, allow the mixture to stand for 5 minutes, then spread half of it on to the surface of one of the cakes and

Coconut Lime Cake

scatter with half the lime zest. Place the other cake on top, spread the rest of the icing on top of that and scatter the rest of the zest over. Then place the cake in the fridge for 30 minutes to firm up the icing before serving.

———— ◊ ————

Pile-it-High Orange *and* Rhubarb Meringue Pie

.

SERVES 6–8

The flavour of orange zest does something quite magical to the flavour of rhubarb, and this light, fluffy meringue pie is a perfect dessert for late spring. 'Pile-it-high meringue', incidentally, applies only if you have extra egg whites to use up or want *to make the meringue high. If not, you can simply use the egg whites in the recipe: it will still be superb!*

FOR THE PASTRY:
6 oz (175 g) plain flour
1½ oz (40 g) butter or margarine
1½ oz (40 g) lard
cold water to mix

FOR THE FILLING:
1½ lb (700 g) rhubarb
grated zest and juice of 3 oranges
3 oz (75 g) caster sugar
3 level tablespoons cornflour
3 egg yolks

FOR THE MERINGUE:
3 large egg whites (minimum)

6 oz (175 g) caster sugar
or
you can use as many egg whites as you have:
4 egg whites need 8 oz (225 g) sugar,
5 need 10 oz (275 g) sugar,
6 need 12 oz (350 g) sugar

You will also need a 9-in (23-cm) quiche tin, 1¼ inches (3 cm) deep, lightly greased, and a baking-sheet.

Pre-heat the oven to gas mark 5, 375°F (190°C), and pre-heat the baking-sheet as well.

Begin by making the pastry: rub the fats into the flour and add enough cold water to make a smooth dough that leaves the bowl clean. Then wrap it in a polythene bag and leave it in the fridge for 30 minutes to rest and become more elastic. Meanwhile wash and trim the rhubarb and cut it into chunks, place it in a shallow baking-dish and sprinkle in the grated orange zest followed by the sugar.

Take the pastry from the fridge, roll it out to a round (giving it quarter-turns as you do so) and use it to line the tin, pressing it up a little way above the edge of the tin. Next prick the base all over with a fork and use some of the egg yolks to paint all over the base and sides to provide a seal. Put the tin on the pre-heated baking-sheet on a high shelf in the oven and place the rhubarb on the lowest shelf. The pastry should take about 20–25 minutes to brown and crisp, and the rhubarb about 25–30 minutes to become soft. Then remove them from the oven.

While you're waiting for that you can squeeze the orange juice into a small saucepan. Use a little of it to mix the cornflour to a smooth paste in a bowl, then bring the rest up to simmering point. Next pour the hot orange juice on to the cornflour mixture and pour the whole lot back into the saucepan, then whisk over the heat with a small balloon whisk till it becomes very thick indeed, then remove it from the heat.

Now strain the cooked rhubarb over a bowl, then add the rhubarb juices and the egg yolks to the cornflour mixture and, still whisking, bring it up to the boil again. Remove from the heat, tip the strained rhubarb into the bowl and stir it into the cornflour mixture.

Now, for the meringue, put the egg whites into a large, roomy bowl and, using an electric hand-whisk, beat them until they reach the stage where, when you lift the whisk, little peaks stand up and just slightly turn over. Next beat the sugar in, 1 tablespoon at a time, whisking well after each addition. Pour the rhubarb mixture into the pastry shell, then spoon the meringue mixture over, making sure that it covers the edges of the pastry with no gaps. Then just pile it on, 'normal', high or very high. Place the pie on the centre shelf of the oven, at the same temperature as before, and bake it for 25 minutes or until the outside of the meringue is golden. Remove it from the oven and leave for about 2 hours before serving.

——————— ◊ ———————

Hazelnut Shortbread *with* Summer Fruits

·

SERVES 8

T*hese are whisper-thin rounds of hazelnut shortcake which make a crunchy contrast to the sharpness of summer fruits. The best way to fill them is to make a summer fruit coulis (sauce) and combine this with a mixture of whole summer fruits – and if you want to go the whole hog, some chilled pouring cream will make it sensational.*

FOR THE HAZELNUT SHORTBREAD:	FOR THE FRUIT COULIS:
5 oz (150 g) softened butter	4 oz (110 g) redcurrants
5 oz (150 g) plain flour	4 oz (110 g) strawberries
2½ oz (60 g) rice flour	2 oz (50 g) raspberries
2½ oz (60 g) icing sugar	2 oz (50 g) sugar
3 oz (75 g) hazelnuts	icing sugar for dusting

FOR THE FRUIT FILLING:	
4 oz (110 g) redcurrants	**You will also need 2 large, solid baking-sheets, lightly greased, and a 3½-inch (9-cm) round pastry cutter.**
4 oz (110 g) blackcurrants	
8 oz (225 g) raspberries	
8 oz (225 g) strawberries	
2 level tablespoons sugar	Pre-heat the oven to gas mark 4, 350°F (180°C).

For the shortbreads you first need to lightly toast the hazelnuts by spreading them out on a heatproof plate and popping them into the oven for 10 minutes. Then, to remove their papery skins, you rub them in a tea-towel or between sheets of kitchen paper. Then place them in a food processor and process to grind them down finely until they look rather like ground almonds.

Now in a mixing-bowl cream the butter and sugar together until light and fluffy, then gradually work in the sifted flours, followed by the hazelnuts, bringing the mixture together to a stiff ball. Next place the dough in a polythene bag and leave it in the fridge to rest for 30 minutes. After that transfer it to a flat surface and roll it out to a thickness of about ¼ inch (5 mm), then stamp out sixteen rounds by placing the cutter on the pastry and just giving it a sharp tap (don't twist it at all: simply lift the cutter and the piece will drop out).

Arrange all the biscuits on the baking-sheets and lightly prick each one with a fork. Bake them for 10–12 minutes or until light brown. Cool on the baking-sheet for about 10 minutes, then remove to a wire rack to cool completely.

For the fruit filling, strip the redcurrants and blackcurrants into a saucepan, add the sugar, then place on a medium heat and let them cook for

3–4 minutes or until the juice begins to run. Transfer them to a bowl and, when they're quite cold, gently stir in the raspberries and strawberries.

The coulis is made simply by soaking the fruits in the sugar for 30 minutes, then liquidising or processing them to make a smooth sauce, then passing it through a sieve to extract the pips.

Just before serving gently fold the whole fruits into the sauce and use the mixture to sandwich the hazelnut biscuits together, then dust with icing sugar before taking to the table.

◊

Equipment Update

I never cease to be amazed at the poor quality of so many items of equipment that are supposed to be of use to people who cook but that actually turn out to be a liability. Cheap and trashy kitchen equipment that does not do the job it claims to do has to be replaced, making it far more expensive in the long run.

I also know from the letters I receive that quality kitchen shops are not to be found in every area – so let me say two things. First, when you *do* find a good kitchen equipment shop, please support it – we need it. Second, don't despair: if there isn't one near you, there are mail-order firms that can help (see opposite for addresses).

Cooking can be hard at the best of times, but if you don't have good equipment it's ten times harder. In the *Complete Illustrated Cookery Course* I have written a very comprehensive list of basic equipment, but here I would like to add one or two items that are new and may be useful.

SPATULA
My best discovery recently has been a simple spatula called Rubber Maid (from Divertimenti; see opposite). Many spatulas do the job well, but this one does it brilliantly – it even scrapes out scrambled eggs. The secret, I think, is in its spoon shape. It comes in various sizes and I would recommend you invest in a small, medium *and* large one. You won't be sorry.

ROASTING-TRAYS AND TINS
It has long been fashionable to serve grilled vegetables in restaurants but unlike catering grills domestic ones are not suitable, making the whole process too fiddly. I have now experimented successfully with oven-roasting vegetables, which gives the same charred, concentrated flavour without the fuss. This, though, involves using a very high oven temperature which in turn calls for extremely solid roasting-trays (which need to have shallow sides to prevent the vegetables steaming). Some ovens have a built-in solid shelf with shallow sides which does the job perfectly, but, if not, I have discovered a roasting-tin made by a British firm called Mermaid. The sides are 2 cm deep, the quality is excellent and the tray can be used in winter for roasting potatoes, etc. Order this from your local kitchen shop or from Divertimenti (see opposite).

MINI MUFFIN TINS
If you have difficulty obtaining mini muffin tins or midi (man-sized) muffin tins or the appropriate paper cases, they are available from Lakeland Plastics (see opposite).

FLAME PROOF TERRACOTTA COOKING-DISH
Another lovely piece of equipment we came across when we were filming the television series is a round flameproof terracotta cooking-dish with shallow sides and handles. Yes, it really is flameproof – provided you don't subject it to sudden and extreme changes of temperature, such as removing it from the hot stove to cold water or vice versa. The joy is that something like Chicken with Sherry Vinegar and Tarragon Sauce can be cooked and served in the same lovely terracotta dish, which cuts washing up greasy pans to a minimum. We've used it in the oven too, for Sliced Potatoes Baked with Tomatoes and Basil, and it's very much in keeping with the latest trend in informal entertaining with its simple rustic feel.

OLIVE STONER
Summer readily conjures up visions of Mediterranean food – even if it rains, we can dream – and while we were working on the series I found my hitherto redundant olive stoner suddenly coming into its own.

I feel it now has a starring role in the kitchen because, while the tinned ready-pitted olives are a good store-cupboard stand-by, they are no substitute for the original thing.

ICE-CREAM MAKER

For all through the year, not just the summer, I feel a good investment is an ice-cream maker. If you are likely to make ice cream on a regular basis, it does cut down on the work involved quite substantially. In the relevant chapter (see page 154) I go into more detail, so read that and make up your own mind.

ICE-CREAM SCOOP

On the same subject, an ice-cream scoop is also very useful, and I favour the plain solid aluminium ones. The secret of successful scooping is to store ice cream in long shallow polythene boxes, then run the scoop along the whole length and get perfect new scoops every time.

SELF-LIGHTING BARBECUE CHARCOAL

One of the hit-or-miss aspects of my summer barbecues in the past has been lighting the charcoal. Now, thank goodness, all that worry is ended – with the arrival of self-lighting charcoal. It comes in large boxes yielding two sealed brown-paper bags. What you do is place one entire bag on the barbecue and light the touch paper. Come back in half an hour and, hey presto, the coals are at just the right temperature.

FISH GRILL

Fish is delicious cooked over charcoal, but life is so much easier if you use a fish grill, which dispenses with all that delicate turning over that sometimes succeeds only in breaking the fish. A wire fish-shaped double-sided grill which holds the fish tight in the centre allows you to turn them over as often as you like and still keep them intact. There is also a special one for sardines (see page 89), a bit on the expensive side but worth it if you are as hooked on grilled sardines as we are.

HEAT DIFFUSER

Finally a small gadget that is useful if you have one of those infuriating hobs that won't give a *really* gentle simmer, so the food catches and scorches. It is called a heat diffuser. All you do is place it directly on the gas or the electric plate and it cuts down the heat reaching the pan.

MAIL ORDER ADDRESSES

Divertimenti
www.divertimenti.co.uk
45–47 Wigmore Street
London W1H 9LE
Telephone 020 7935 0689
sales@divertimenti.co.uk
Mail order available

Lakeland Limited
www.lakelandlimited.co.uk
Telephone 01539 488100
net.shop@lakelandlimited.co.uk
Mail order available and outlets nationwide

◊

CHAPTER ELEVEN

SUMMER PRESERVES

◊

One of the recurring joys of summer for me is saving a little bit of it for the winter. On a grey winter day, as you spread Fresh Apricot Preserve (page 204) on your toasted crumpet you can recall – almost smell – that lovely basket of apricots warm and glowing in the sun (see the photograph on pages 132–3). Most of the soft-fruit preserves are in the *Complete Illustrated Cookery Course*, so this time I've introduced a new preserve, one made with gooseberries and elderflower – wonderful spread on freshly made scones!

As for pickles, peaches have proved very versatile. They're great at Christmas served with ham and cold cuts, or if you warm them a little they go particularly well with roast pork or duck, and for vegetarians they make an excellent accompaniment to the savoury cheesecake on page 104. This year's star chutney is made with runner beans: in fact it is the only way to preserve them as they don't freeze at all well. So still to have a taste of them in the winter is a joy. Finally Italian sun-dried tomatoes are rapidly becoming a regular store-cupboard item: if you have a glut of home-grown tomatoes you may not be able to dry them in the Calabrian sunshine, but you *can* dry them in a domestic oven and store them in olive oil. The results are very good and a lot less expensive.

Preceding page: Spiced Pickled Runner Beans (see page 203)

Sweet Pickled Cucumber Slices

·

MAKES 4–5 LB (1.8–2.25 KG)

This is a marvellous pickle to serve as an accompaniment to plain grilled fish or cold cuts – or, best of all, with pâté and toast as a snack.

3 large cucumbers	**¼ level teaspoon ground cloves**
3 large onions	**1 tablespoon mustard seeds**
2 oz (50 g) salt	
1 pint (570 ml) white wine vinegar	
1 lb (450 g) soft brown sugar	**You will also need 4–5 × 1 lb (450 g)**
½ level teaspoon turmeric	**sterilised jars.**

First of all thinly slice the cucumbers, leaving the skins on, and then thinly slice the onions. Now take a large colander and layer the cucumbers and onions in it, sprinkling each layer with salt. Then place a suitably-sized plate over them and press it down with a heavy weight. Place the colander over a dish or bowl to catch the escaping juice and leave it like that for 3 hours. Then pour off or squeeze out as much liquid as possible.

Now put the vinegar, sugar and spices into a large saucepan and stir over a medium heat until the sugar has completely dissolved. Next add the drained cucumber and onion slices, bring it all up to the boil and simmer (uncovered) for *1 minute* only. Remove the pan from the heat and, using a draining-spoon, spoon the cucumber and onion into jars. Next boil the spiced vinegar mixture (again uncovered) for 15 minutes and then pour it into the warmed sterilised jars. Seal the jars and label when cold. Store for a month before serving. NOTE: To prepare the jars, wash them thoroughly in warm soapy water, rinse and put them in a cool oven to dry and get warm.

◊

Preserved Pickled Peaches (or Nectarines)

·

MAKES 1¾ PINTS (1 LITRE)

*W*hen *there's a glut of peaches going for a song on the market, that's the time to pickle some to keep for the winter. They are lovely served with hot baked ham, roast pork or duck. If you're a vegetarian, these peaches and the savoury cheesecake on page 104 make a very good combination. The recipe works well for nectarines too.*

8 large ripe but firm peaches	**1 dessertspoon mixed peppercorns**
12 oz (350 g) granulated sugar	**3 shallots, peeled and finely sliced**
1 pint (570 ml) white wine vinegar	
2 tablespoons fresh lime juice	**You will also need a 1¾-pint (1-litre) preserving-jar, sterilised as described on page 199.**
1 dessertspoon coriander seeds	

Begin by measuring the sugar, wine vinegar, lime juice, coriander seeds, peppercorns and shallots into a large saucepan or preserving-pan. Give everything a hefty stir, then place the pan on a low heat and allow to heat through, stirring from time to time until all the sugar has dissolved – don't let it come up to simmering point until all the granules of sugar have completely dissolved.

While that's happening put another saucepan of water on to boil. Then halve the peaches (by slitting them all round with a knife and twisting them in half), remove the stones and drop the peach halves into the boiling water, a few at a time, just for a few seconds. Remove them with a draining-spoon and you should find that the skins slip off easily.

Now place the skinned peach halves in the vinegar and sugar mixture, bring it up to simmering point and gently poach the fruit for 15 minutes or until tender when tested with a skewer. Use a draining-spoon to remove the peaches and transfer them to the warmed preserving-jar. Now boil the syrup rapidly to reduce it to approximately half its original volume, then pour it through a strainer over the peaches. If you have any syrup left, reserve it as you will find that after about 24 hours the peaches will have absorbed some of their syrup and you can use the rest to top up. Seal the jar and keep for 6 weeks before using.

———————— ◊ ————————

Preserved Pickled Peaches

Pickled Limes

·

MAKES ENOUGH TO FILL AN 18 FL OZ (500 ML) PRESERVING-JAR

This is a very sharp, concentrated preserve which goes wonderfully with fish, especially crab cakes (page 48). It is also good with the Baked Thai Red Curry Chicken on page 122 – but because it's so strong very little is needed.

12–14 fresh limes
5 level dessertspoons salt
9 oz (250 g) granulated sugar
12 whole cloves
12 whole black peppercorns
4 fl oz (110 ml) water

You will also need a non-metallic tray measuring about 15 × 10 inches (37.5 × 25 cm) and an 18 fl oz (500 ml) preserving-jar, sterilised as described on page 199.

You need to begin this recipe the night before, as the limes have to be salted to extract their bitterness. To do this, slice off and discard the ends of 6 of the limes, then cut into slices (skin and all) about ⅛ inch (3 mm) thick. Now spread a layer of kitchen paper all over the non-metallic tray and lay the slices of lime on it in a single layer with no overlapping. Sprinkle half the salt over the limes, leave them like that for a few hours, then turn them over and sprinkle the rest of the salt over the other side. Cover loosely with another layer of kitchen paper and leave in the fridge overnight.

Next day rinse the lime slices in a colander, sluicing and turning them under a cold running tap until all traces of salt have been washed away. Now transfer them to a saucepan with just enough water to cover them, then simmer very gently for about 30–45 minutes or until the slices are very tender (watch this carefully after 30 minutes are up, otherwise it's possible that they can overcook and turn to mush: the slices need to be tender but still intact).

Now squeeze the juice from the other limes – you need 7 fl oz (200 ml) in all and sometimes this can mean 6 limes, sometimes 7 or 8, depending on their size and juiciness. Place the juice in a saucepan along with 4 fl oz (110 ml) water, the sugar and spices, stir over a gentle heat until the sugar has dissolved completely, then simmer very gently for 25 minutes without a lid. The liquid will reduce slightly, but do keep an eye on it as it mustn't boil rapidly or it will tend to caramelise.

Then remove the syrup from the heat and take out the spices using a draining-spoon. Now add the drained lime slices to the syrup and pour the whole lot into the warmed sterilised jar. Seal it down, label when cold and keep for a month before eating.

◊

Spiced Pickled Runner Beans

.

MAKES APPROX. 6 LB (2.75 KG)

This recipe was given to me by Kathleen Field from Bungay in Suffolk, and was first published in the Food Aid Cookbook *in 1986. She said then, 'There comes a time in late summer when the family say, "Oh, not more runner beans again." Well, they must be picked, and here's what to do with them.' We've been doing just that with ours each year since then and the chutney is now a firm favourite. Thanks, Kathleen!*

2 lb (900 g) runner beans (weighed after trimming and slicing)	**1 rounded tablespoon turmeric**
	8 oz (225 g) soft brown sugar
1½ lb (700 g) onions, chopped	**1 lb (450 g) demerara sugar**
1½ pints (850 ml) malt vinegar	
1½ oz (40 g) cornflour	**You will also need 6 × 1 lb (450 g) jars,**
1 heaped tablespoon mustard powder	**sterilised as described on page 199.**

First of all put the chopped onions into a preserving-pan or large casserole or saucepan with 10 fl oz (275 ml) of the vinegar. Bring them up to simmering point and let them simmer gently for about 20 minutes or until the onions are soft.

Meanwhile cook the sliced beans in boiling salted water for 5 minutes, then strain them in a colander and add to the onions. Now in a small basin mix the cornflour, mustard and turmeric with a little of the remaining vinegar – enough to make a smooth paste – then add this paste to the onion mixture. Pour in the rest of the vinegar and simmer everything for 10 minutes. After that stir in both quantities of sugar until they dissolve and continue to simmer for a further 15 minutes. Then pot the pickle in warmed sterilised jars and seal and label when cold. Keep for at least a month before eating.

— ◊ —

Fresh Apricot Preserve

·

MAKES 3–4 LB (1.35 KG–1.8 KG)

T*his is my mother's recipe, and every year she waits patiently for the price of apricots to come down – which usually happens in August, especially at the end of a warm summer day when whole boxes are sold off at the markets by stallholders at bargain prices.*

2 lb (900 g) fresh apricots	**You will also need 3–4 × 1 lb (450 g)**
2 lb (900 g) granulated sugar	**preserving-jars, sterilised as**
juice of 1 large lemon	**described on page 199.**
a trace of butter	

Begin this the night before you actually want to make the jam. Take a large casserole or small preserving-pan and grease the base with a smear of butter to prevent the preserve sticking. Halve the apricots (reserving the stones) and place them in layers in the pan, sprinkling the sugar in between the layers. Add the lemon juice, then cover with a cloth and leave them overnight – this pre-soaking in sugar firms up the fruit and this will ensure that the apricot pieces stay intact when you come to make the jam. At the same time crack approximately half the apricot stones with a nutcracker and remove the kernels. Now blanch them in boiling water for 1–2 minutes, then drain and dry them and slip off their skins. Reserve the kernels to add to the preserve later.

To make the preserve, first pop three tea-plates into the fridge (this is for testing the set), then place the pan over a medium heat and let the sugar melt and completely dissolve – about 15 minutes. The sugar must be absolutely clear and free of granules, otherwise the preserve will be sugary. When the sugar has dissolved turn the heat up to its very highest and let the mixture boil very rapidly for about 10–20 minutes, stirring from time to time to prevent sticking.

After that use the cold tea-plates to test for a set. Remove the pan from the heat and place a teaspoonful of the preserve onto one of the tea-plates. Allow it to cool for a few seconds, then push it with your finger: if a crinkly skin has formed on the jam, then it has set. If it hasn't set, boil it again for another 5 minutes and do another test. When you have a set, remove the preserve from the heat and stir in a trace of butter which will disperse any scum that has formed. Then add the reserved kernels and let it settle for 15 minutes before pouring it into warmed sterilised jars. Seal while still warm and label the jars when cold.

———————— ◇ ————————

Fresh Apricot Preserve

Gooseberry *and* Elderflower Preserve

·

MAKES 3 LB (1.35 KG)

Was it a happy accident, or nature's clever plan, that while English gooseberries are ripe and ready for picking, the elderflower trees are in full blossom, and that the flavours of the two together are superlative? Now that elderflower is concentrated in a cordial, combining them is so much easier and makes one of the nicest of summer preserves.

2 lb (900 g) gooseberries
2 lb (900 g) granulated sugar
5 fl oz (150 ml) water
4 tablespoons elderflower cordial
a trace of butter

You will also need 3 × 1 lb (450 g) jam jars, sterilised as described on page 199, and 3–4 tea-plates chilled in the fridge (for testing).

First of all take a large, heavy saucepan and smear the base with a butter paper as this will help prevent the preserve sticking at a high temperature. Then top and tail the gooseberries into the pan and add the water. Next bring up to simmering point and simmer very gently until the fruit is tender – this will take about 15 minutes.

After that add the sugar and stir well, then, keeping the heat low, wait for the sugar to dissolve completely (about 15 minutes), testing the liquid with a wooden spoon to make sure that there are no little granules of sugar left. Now turn the heat up to its very highest setting and let the preserve boil rapidly for 8 minutes, then take it off the heat to test for a set. If it is not set, boil for 5 more minutes and repeat until the preserve is set as described on page 150. When set, stir in the elderflower cordial and allow it to settle for 15 minutes before pouring it into warmed sterilised jars. Seal with waxed discs, put the lids on and label when cold.

———————— ◊ ————————

Preserved Dried Tomatoes

·

MAKES 3 × 10 FL OZ (275 ML) JARS OR 1 × 1¾ (1 LITRE) JAR

If you grow your own tomatoes, or can get hold of a good quantity when they're going cheap, it really is worth preserving them for use in the winter. Although they're not dried in the Italian sunshine like the imported kind, we have found that the oven-dried variety still have a lovely concentrated flavour.

6 lb (2.6 kg) ripe but firm, medium-sized tomatoes

3 level teaspoons salt

1 pint (570 ml) extra virgin olive oil with a hint of basil

You will also need 3 × 10 fl oz (275 ml) jars or 1 × 1¾ pint (1 litre) jar, sterilised as described on page 199, and 2 wire cooling-trays.

Pre-heat the oven to gas mark ½, 175°F (80°C).

Begin by washing the tomatoes and removing the stalks, then slice them in half across the middle, turn the cut side down on a plate and squeeze out the seeds. Lay some double layers of kitchen paper on a work-surface and leave each half upside down on them to drain while you get on with preparing the rest.

When they're all ready, turn them over and very lightly sprinkle the insides with salt – don't overdo this or you will lose the lovely concentrated sweetness when the tomatoes are dried. Now lay the tomatoes, cut side down, on the wire cooling-trays, leaving just enough space between them so that they do not touch. Next lay some foil on the bottom shelf to catch any drips and save on oven cleaning, then place the two racks in the oven, leaving space for the air to circulate freely between the shelves.

As you close the door wedge it with a skewer (or something similar) to stop it closing completely – it needs only about ¼-inch (5-mm) gap, just sufficient to stop the build-up of heat so that the tomatoes dry rather than cook.

If the tomatoes are of medium size they will probably need 8 hours to dry completely, but take a look at them after 6 hours and remove any which appear to be ready. At this stage you can turn them the other way up. What you want are the tomatoes to be dried but still retaining a slight fleshy feel – don't let them go too papery. If in doubt, taste one: they should be chewy and the flavour a concentrated tomato sweetness.

Have ready the jar(s), clean and sterilised. When the tomatoes are cool pack them into the jar(s) – not too tightly – and top up with the oil before sealing and labelling.

NOTE: We have stored these for 6 months and they have kept beautifully.

◊

CHAPTER TWELVE

BREAD, PIZZA *and* FOCACCIA

———— ◊ ————

Summer, when the weather is hot and energy levels are low, is perhaps not the best time to be baking bread. The last thing I feel like doing is kneading dough in a hot kitchen on a sunny day. However, we *are* talking about the English summer, and the truth is that we can always count on a fair (or unfair!) proportion of colder, rainy days – in which case a spot of bread-making can be very therapeutic and comforting.

There's another good reason for making the breads in this chapter: all of them have a variety of ingredients and flavours, and while we're all struggling to do without butter it makes life much more interesting if the bread itself has its own individuality and interest to compensate for the lack of butter. So find a chilly day and bake a batch of flavoured breads for the freezer: if you make sticks or rolls you can just take a few out as and when you need them.

NOTES ON BREAD-MAKING

I have gone into this subject in some detail in the *Complete Illustrated Cookery Course*, but for the beginner the following notes may be helpful.

Easy-blend Yeast

Yeast is what enables bread to rise, and easy-blend has more or less superseded the fresh and dried varieties. All you do with this is sprinkle the required amount in with the flour and add the water separately. Each 1 lb (450 g) flour needs 2 level teaspoons of easy-blend yeast – exactly the same as 2 level teaspoons of dried yeast. But a warning: do inspect the date stamp carefully, as easy-blend will not do its work once it becomes stale.

Kneading

Where kneading is necessary, simply place the dough on a flat work-surface and stretch it away from you, using the heel of one hand to push from the middle and the clenched knuckles of your other hand to pull the other half of the dough towards you – both hands should move simultaneously to stretch out the dough. Then lift the edges over and back to the middle. Give it a quarter-turn and repeat the process. It soon becomes a rather rhythmic operation, and the dough will then start to become very elastic. This is the gluten at work. In simple terms the water meets the gluten and what makes it become springy and alive is a good pummelling. A properly kneaded piece of dough will look plump and rounded with a very smooth surface.

Rising

The dough must be left to rise for a specified period to allow the yeast to do its work: all yeast doughs need at least an hour at room temperature before baking, or less in a warm place which does speed up the rising. I use the plate-warming compartment of my cooker, but some may be too hot for this and care has to be taken because too high a temperature can kill off the yeast. Always cover the dough, either with a folded damp tea-towel or with clingfilm. When properly risen dough should have doubled in size and should spring back and feel very slightly sticky when lightly touched with the finger. Remember that the longer the rising time, the more uniformly the yeast will work and the more evenly textured the finished bread will be.

Knocking Down and Proving

Some recipes call for a second rising or 'proving', which is exactly what it is: the yeast proving that it is still alive and active. The proving ensures there will be an even rise. Knocking down is simply punching all the gas out of the dough and bringing it back to its original size, to allow it to rise for a second time in the bread tin.

Baking

Bread tins should always be greased generously. I use butter for this and spread it evenly round the tins with a piece of kitchen paper. Always bake bread in a hot oven, and bear in mind it's always better to over-cook rather than under-cook bread. To test if a loaf is cooked, tap it on the under-side with your knuckles, and if it sounds hollow, it's done. If you like very crusty bread, after you've turned the loaves out of their tins, pop them back in the oven upside down for 5–10 minutes.

Cooling

Always cool bread on a wire cooling-tray. If you place it directly on a flat surface, the steam will be trapped and you'll find that the crust will become soggy. Also a loaf that has not been properly cooled before freezing or storing can taste doughy.

BREAD, PIZZA *AND* FOCACCIA

Mini Focaccia Bread *with* Four Toppings

·

MAKES 1 LARGE OR 4 MINI FOCACCIA

Focaccia is an Italian flat bread made with olive oil. The flavour of the oil is important, so it's advisable to use a good, strong, fruity virgin olive oil for this. What's good about focaccia is that it gives you scope to invent all kinds of interesting toppings. Below I've given the basic recipe for making either one full-size focaccia or four mini ones. You can also vary the toppings – that is, if you cut the topping ingredients down to a quarter of the original quantity, you can have four minis with a different topping on each (as in the photograph opposite).

FOR THE BASIC FOCACCIA DOUGH:	2 teaspoons easy-blend yeast
12 oz (350 g) plain white flour	7½ fl oz (210 ml) warm water
½ teaspoon salt	1½ tablespoons extra virgin olive oil

Begin by sifting the flour and salt into a large mixing-bowl, then sprinkle in the yeast and mix that in. Next pour in the warm water along with 1½ tablespoons of olive oil and mix everything to a dough that leaves the sides of the bowl clean (if necessary you can add a few more drops of water). Now turn the dough out on to a lightly floured surface and knead it for about 10 minutes (alternatively you can use an electric mixer with a dough hook and process for 5 minutes).

When the dough feels very bouncy and elastic, return it to the bowl, cover with clingfilm and leave in a warm place until it has doubled in size (about 1½ hours or more depending on the heat in the kitchen: if there's no suitable warm place you can sit the bowl over a saucepan of warm water – but not over direct heat). After that turn the dough out on to the work-surface and punch the air out by kneading it again for 2–3 minutes. Now it's ready for a topping.

If you're making a full-sized focaccia, pat the dough out into an approximate oval shape 12 × 10 inches (30 × 25 cm), arrange your chosen topping over (or into) the whole thing and proceed as described on page 214 – except that the large focaccia will take 25–30 minutes to cook.

——————— ◊ ———————

Clockwise from the top: Mini Focaccia Bread with Rock-salt Topping; Blue Cheese, Garlic and Thyme Topping; Red Onion, Olive and Rosemary Topping; Basil and Sun-dried Tomato Topping (pages 214–6)

Red Onion, Olive *and* Rosemary Topping

·

MAKES ENOUGH FOR 1 LARGE OR 4 MINI FOCACCIA

2 small red onions, halved and then sliced into ¼-inch (5-mm) wedges	**4 teaspoons chopped fresh rosemary**
	1 tablespoon olive oil
4 oz (110 g) pitted black olives, halved	**1 teaspoon rock salt**

Take two-thirds of the olives and push them evenly into the dough, then divide the dough into four and place the sections on an oiled baking-sheet, then use your hands to pat out each piece into a sort of oblong, rounded at the ends and measuring 4 × 3 inches (10 × 7.5 cm). Next sprinkle a quarter of the remaining olives and a quarter of the rosemary and onions on to each piece. Finally sprinkle the surface with rock salt and drizzle the olive oil all over each focaccia. Cover with a damp tea-towel and leave the dough to puff up again for 30 minutes.

Meanwhile pre-heat the oven to gas mark 5, 375°F (190°C). When the 30 minutes are up, bake the breads in the oven for about 15 minutes or until they are golden round the edges and look well cooked in the centre. Cool on a wire rack and serve warm.

———— ◊ ————

Rock-salt Topping

·

MAKES ENOUGH FOR 1 LARGE OR 4 MINI FOCACCIA

4 teaspoons crushed rock salt	**1 tablespoon olive oil**

Divide the dough into four, put the pieces on an oiled baking-sheet and pull and push each one into shape as described above. Then drizzle the olive oil over the surface of each one and sprinkle the rock salt over. Cover with a damp tea-towel and leave for 30 minutes for the dough to puff up. Meanwhile pre-heat the oven to gas mark 5, 375°F (190°C), and bake the focaccias for about 15 minutes. Cool on a wire rack and serve warm.

———— ◊ ————

Blue Cheese, Garlic *and* Thyme Topping

·

MAKES ENOUGH FOR 1 LARGE OR 4 MINI FOCACCIA

6 oz (175 g) gorgonzola cheese	**4 teaspoons fresh thyme leaves**
4 large cloves garlic, cut lengthways into thin matchstick strips	**1 tablespoon olive oil**
	freshly milled black pepper

Divide the dough into four, place the pieces on an oiled baking-sheet and pull and push each one into shape as described on page 214, then cover the surface of each one with the thyme leaves and a fairly liberal grinding of black pepper. Next remove the rind from the gorgonzola and cut the cheese into dice. Sprinkle these over the surface of the four pieces of dough along with the strips of garlic. Now drizzle the olive oil over the surface of the toppings, cover with a damp cloth and leave to puff up again for 30 minutes. Meanwhile pre-heat the oven to gas mark 5, 375°F (190°C), and bake the focaccias for about 15 minutes. Cool on a wire rack and serve warm.

◊

Basil *and* Sun-dried Tomato Topping

·

MAKES ENOUGH FOR 1 LARGE OR 4 MINI FOCACCIA

approx. 24 fresh basil leaves	**1 teaspoon rock salt**
2 oz (50 g) sun-dried tomatoes preserved in oil, drained and chopped small	**1 tablespoon olive oil**

First take 12 of the basil leaves and tear them into small pieces, then push them evenly into the dough. Divide the dough into four pieces, place them on an oiled baking-sheet and pull and push them into shape (as described on page 214). Gently push the sun-dried tomatoes into the surface of each piece of dough. Next sprinkle the remaining whole basil leaves on to the dough along with the rock salt and finally drizzle the olive oil over the surface of the topping. Cover with a damp tea-towel and leave for 30 minutes for the dough to puff up. Meanwhile pre-heat the oven to gas mark 5, 375°F (190°C), and bake the focaccias for about 15 minutes. Cool on a wire rack and serve warm.

◊

Sun-dried Tomato *and* Ricotta Bread

·

MAKES 12 ROLLS OR 30 BREADSTICKS

This is a lovely, moist bread which I like to make into individual rolls or breadsticks. The latter are great to munch on at a supper party while everyone is waiting for the first course.

12 oz (350 g) white soft-grain flour	**1 oz (25 g) sun-dried tomatoes preserved in oil, drained and chopped small**
1 level teaspoon salt	
1½ level teaspoons easy-blend yeast	**2 tablespoons olive oil (from the tomatoes if possible)**
5 fl oz (150 ml) warm water	
4 oz (110 g) ricotta cheese, at room temperature	**1½ tablespoons chopped fresh basil leaves**

First take a large, roomy bowl and sift the flour into it (this will mean that the grains will still be sitting in the sieve, so just return them to the flour). Now sprinkle in the easy-blend yeast, the salt, tomatoes and basil and mix well. After that make a well in the centre of the mixture, measure 5 fl oz (150 ml) of hand-hot water, pour it into the flour and begin to mix it a little. Then add the cheese and olive oil and finish the mixing till you have a smooth dough.

Now knead the dough for 5 minutes or until it becomes springy and elastic (this can be done in a mixer or a food processor with a dough-kneading attachment). After that cover the bowl with clingfilm and leave the dough to prove till doubled in size – I can't give a timing on this because it depends on the kitchen temperature, but don't hurry it as the bread will be better if it has a longer proving time (see page 211).

When it has doubled in size, remove the dough from the bowl on to lightly floured surface and punch it down to release all the air. Now you can shape it either into twelve rolls, knots, cottage shapes or plain rounds, or into breadsticks: use ½ oz (10 g) quantities rolled out into fat pencil shapes, then slash diagonally with a knife so that they look like miniature French sticks. You should get thirty of these in all. Arrange the rolls or sticks on separate greased baking-sheets, cover with clingfilm and leave to rise once more to double in size.

Meanwhile pre-heat the oven to gas mark 7, 425°F (220°C). Bake the rolls for 18–20 minutes, or the breadsticks for 10–12 minutes. Cool on a wire cooling-tray. These will freeze well in sealed polythene freezer bags.

———————— ◊ ————————

Green Peppercorn Bread

·

MAKES 15 ROLLS OR 50 BREADSTICKS

This is a lovely, gutsy, spicy bread.

1 lb (450 g) strong white bread flour

2 level teaspoons salt

2 level teaspoons easy-blend yeast

10 fl oz (275 ml) warm water

1 level tablespoon dried green peppercorns, crushed in a pestle and mortar

3 tablespoons extra virgin olive oil

You will also need 2 solid baking sheets.

Begin by sifting the flour into a large bowl, then sprinkle in the easy-blend yeast and the salt, make a well in the centre and pour in 10 fl oz (275 ml) of hand-hot water. Begin to mix a little, then add the crushed peppercorns and olive oil and continue mixing until you have a smooth dough. Now knead the dough for 5 minutes or until it becomes springy and elastic, and after that cover the bowl with clingfilm and leave it to prove till doubled in size – the length of time will depend on the kitchen temperature, but at all events don't rush it because the longer the proving time, the better the bread.

When it has doubled in size, remove the dough from the bowl to a lightly floured surface, then punch it down to release the air. Now you can shape it either into rolls or breadsticks, in which case use ½ oz (10 g) quantities of the dough rolled out into fat pencil shapes, then slashed diagonally with a knife (to resemble miniature French sticks). Arrange them on separate greased baking-sheets, cover with clingfilm and leave to rise once more to double on size.

Meanwhile pre-heat the oven to gas mark 7, 425°F (220°C). Bake the rolls for 18–20 minutes, or the breadsticks for 10–12 minutes. Cool on a wire cooling-tray. Both freeze successfully in sealed polythene freezer bags.

———— ◊ ————

Wholegrain Bread *with* Sunflower *and* Poppy Seeds

·

MAKES 2 × 1 LB (450 G) LOAVES

I love the flavour and nutty texture of this loaf which, when it's a couple of days old, toasts really well – lovely with some home-made preserves for breakfast and so good there's no need for butter!

1 lb (450 g) wholemeal flour	**4 oz (110 g) sunflower seeds**
2 level teaspoons salt	**1 oz (25 g) poppy seeds**
2 level teaspoons easy-blend yeast	
12 fl oz (350 ml) hand-hot water	
1 dessertspoon cane molasses sugar	**You will also need 2 × 1 lb (450 g) loaf**
2 tablespoons olive oil	**tins, well buttered.**

First of all sift the flour and salt together into a large bowl (returning the grains left in the sieve to the flour), then sprinkle in the yeast and give a good stir to mix it in. Next add the sunflower and poppy seeds and mix again. Now dissolve the sugar in the water, pour this over the flour together with the oil and mix everything to a dough. Knead it well for 5 minutes, then cover the bowl with clingfilm and leave it to rise until doubled in size.

When it has doubled its bulk, turn the dough out on to a lightly floured surface and knead it once again. Now divide the dough into two, pull each piece into a length, fold one edge to the centre and the other on top of that, then place the loaves in the greased tins. Cover and leave to prove again, and meanwhile pre-heat the oven to gas mark 6, 400°F (200°C).

When the dough has risen to the top of the tins, place them in the oven on a highish shelf and bake for 40 minutes. Then turn the loaves out and return them without tins, upside down, to the oven (to crisp the edges) for a further 5 minutes. Then cool on a wire cooling-tray.

———— ◊ ————

Frying-pan Pizza *with* Smoked Mozzarella *and* Sun-dried Tomatoes

·

SERVES 2 AS A MAIN COURSE OR 4 AS A STARTER

This is the easiest home-made pizza in the world. It's made with a scone dough which happily does not require to be kneaded and proved. The topping can, of course, be varied to include whatever you like best, but the combination below is, I think, one of the nicest. If you don't have time to make up the tomato sauce, you can substitute 4 tablespoons of tomato purée.

FOR THE BASE:

8 oz (225 g) self-raising flour

½ teaspoon salt

freshly milled black pepper

1 tablespoon chopped fresh herbs

4 tablespoons olive oil

water

FOR THE TOPPING:

5 oz (150 g) smoked mozzarella cheese, cut into 1-inch (2.5-cm) pieces

4 oz (110 g) sun-dried tomatoes preserved in oil, drained and chopped

2 tablespoons preserved tomato oil (from the above)

12 black olives, pitted and sliced

2 oz (50 g) mushrooms, sliced

2 tablespoons capers, drained

2 tablespoons torn fresh basil leaves

salt and freshly milled black pepper

FOR THE TOMATO SAUCE:

1 lb (450 g) tomatoes, skinned and chopped

1 small onion, chopped

1 medium clove garlic, crushed

1 tablespoon olive oil

1 dessertspoon chopped fresh basil

salt and freshly milled black pepper

First make up the tomato sauce by heating the olive oil in a small saucepan, adding the onion and garlic and cooking for 2–3 minutes to soften. Then add the chopped tomatoes and basil, season with salt and pepper, and continue to cook over a medium heat for 20–25 minutes until the tomatoes have reduced and concentrated their flavour. (While you're at it, why not make a larger quantity of this – it freezes very well!)

Now for the pizza base: sift the flour into a bowl along with some seasoning and the herbs. Make a well in the centre and pour in 2 tablespoons of the olive oil followed by 4 tablespoons of water. Now mix to a soft (though not sticky) dough – you may find that you have to add a further tablespoon or so of water to get the right consistency.

Next prepare a floured surface, turn the dough out on to it and knead lightly before rolling out to a round to fit the base of a 9–10-inch (23–25-cm) frying-pan. Heat 1 tablespoon of the remaining olive oil in the pan, place the circle of dough in it and cook over a low heat for about 5 minutes or until the base is lightly browned. Have ready an oiled plate and turn the pizza base out on to it. Then, after heating a further tablespoon of the remaining olive oil in the pan, slide the pizza back in and cook the reverse side for 5 minutes.

During this time spread the reduced tomato sauce over the surface of the pizza, then scatter over the pieces of mozzarella, the dried tomatoes, olives, mushrooms, capers and torn basil leaves. Season, then drizzle the oil from the preserved tomatoes over the top. To see if the underside of the pizza is cooked, you can lift up a corner with a palette knife and have a look. When it's ready, transfer the pan to a pre-heated grill for 2–3 minutes to melt the cheese and heat the topping. Serve straight away.

◊

Index

Page numbers in *italic* refer to the photographs